# The National Ballet of Canada

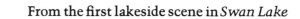

From the first lakeside scene in *Swan Lake*

A posed group shot of the artists

Facing title page, the first act of
*The Sleeping Beauty*

The corps de ballet as the Shades in
*Bayaderka*

A CELEBRATION

WITH
PHOTOGRAPHS
BY KEN BELL

AND
A MEMOIR BY
CELIA FRANCA

# The National Ballet of Canada

UNIVERSITY OF
TORONTO PRESS
Toronto Buffalo London

© University of Toronto Press 1978
Toronto  Buffalo  London

To the memory of Kay Ambrose

**Canadian Cataloguing in Publication Data**

Bell, Ken, 1914-

The National Ballet of Canada

ISBN 0-8020-2303-7
1. National Ballet of Canada – History.
I. Franca, Celia, 1921-    II. Title.
GV1786.N3B44   792.8'0971   C78-001431-6

Publication of this book has been made
possible by grants from the Canada Council
and the Ontario Arts Council

# Contents

The Carnival dance from *Romeo and Juliet*

# Preface

Kay as chief cook and bottle washer and, opposite, as designer and maid of all work

When Ken Bell and I were first discussing the idea of making this book, we both found ourselves talking about Kay Ambrose. Ken thought that we should dedicate this book to her memory – and this we are pleased to do, recalling all the energy and spirit she gave to the National Ballet in its earliest days.

Kay was born in England, became fascinated by the dance, and arrived in Canada soon after the beginnings of the National Ballet. She was author, artist, designer, illustrator, publicist, intellectual, devotee of the dance, friend, chief cook and bottle washer, encourager and sustainer, a human being *par excellence*. She died of cancer in England in 1971.

Few artists or associates, former or present, of the National Ballet of Canada realize the prodigious, often anonymous, contribution made by Kay Ambrose to the company. Without her efforts, indeed, the young company might not have survived and flourished.

She it was who in her enthusiasm introduced Ken to the company as its photographer.

Back in the early fifties, when the company was operating on a shoestring, we needed photos for the newspapers in order to help publicize our productions and increase the awareness of ballet – near to zero as it was – among the people of Canada. Photographs were essential, but they cost money: film, photographer's time, studios, big glossy prints. There should be studio photographs of individual dancers, but there should also be stage scenes to prove that the company could boast full décors, extravagant costumes (even though many were made out of old curtains), and a cast of thousands. The stage scenes could not be taken in a studio, but we had no permanent theatre or even our own rehearsal space, apart from having very little money to pay the dancers for the extra time they had to give to pose for a stage shot.

So what we did for stage shots was to have the crew set the stage as quickly as possible in lieu of rehearsal time. I would pose the principal dancers and the corps de ballet; we'd be cold, tired, anxious about the performance to come that night. Kay and Ken would be at the front of the first balcony, cameras at the ready. We had no PA system, of course, so Kay would scream at me 'Shove Judie two inches to the right' or 'Squash everything in so we don't hit the blacks'. 'Now, get ready, look lively, lots of expression, DON'T MOVE!' I would count 'one, two, three, NOW,' Ken 'fired,' and we'd pray that the shot was a success.

It usually was. Ken became caught up in our single-minded dedication to the art of dance. He worked passionately, skilfully, and, most important, with a love of his subject. Selflessly, he provided for our necessities without thought of – or at least second thought of – remuneration. He didn't even realize that the pictures he was

taking might win him some prestigious awards.

As the fledgling company slowly spread its wings, conditions changed: action photos were taken, magazines became interested, colour photography was greatly improved. Photo calls have become standard events every season – with all their expense: union electricians look after specially augmented lighting effects; overtime can be paid sometimes to carpenters, dancers, dressers; prima ballerinas and 'ballerinos' fret and froth and delay everything while they change their wigs or shoes. The company's directors and administrators try to soothe their ulcers and think up ways to justify the expense to the finance committee.

These conditions are a far cry from the early days, when we needed all the discipline and teamwork and devotion we could muster to avoid any waste and help ourselves survive. Ken made an incalculable contribution then,

just as he has done through the years since, to publicizing and recording all that the National Ballet of Canada has managed to achieve.

So, too, did Kay Ambrose in our crucial first eight or so years. She would have wanted the book to be a tribute to the photographer, her friend as he has become mine. In thanking them both specially, I do not forget, however, my immense gratitude to the many, many others – skilled professionals, volunteers, and friends – who have shared with me for some twenty-five years the burden and the joy of creating the National Ballet of Canada. I only regret that it has been impossible to mention all of them by name. I thank, among many, Victoria Prystawski, my friend and secretary; David Walker, for endless hours of uncomplaining research; and Rik Davidson, my editorial guide and mentor.

CELIA FRANCA

# Before Canada

I remember that, as a girl growing up in London, England, we learned to recite in kindergarten the poem that begins:

> Up the airy mountain,
> Down the rushy glen,
> We daren't go a-hunting
> For fear of little men.

Looking back now, I can well understand how these lines played a part in creating my favourite daydream: I was wearing a long white dress (I later decided it was made of tulle), and translucent wings sprouted from below my shoulder blades. With an ever so subtle and indeed imperceptible thrust from my toes, there I would be, floating in the air for as long as I wished. By gently undulating my smooth, soft, and milk-white arms, I would move among the tree-tops, my large violet eyes (alas! they were small and grey) shining in the moonlight, my head poised on a long neck and raised towards heaven, my torso sinu-ously curved, my insteps arched, my toes pointed...

This dream of ultimate grace and freedom haunted me. I would sit in school designing in my head the dresses suitable for ethereal travel. Before long, however, I discovered that I was not alone in these fantasies: a century or so earlier they had been realized, in so far as it was possible, on the stage of the Opéra in Paris. Marie Taglioni had danced *sur la pointe* in a ballet called *La Sylphide*, wearing a dress like those of my imaginings. But what was most exciting to discover was that there were others in the world still captivated by the idea of being a spirit of the air – a sylph – and that this romantic tradition of dancing was still going on.

As soon as I could, I became a member of the Ballet Rambert and appeared wearing the romantic tutu in a performance of *Les Sylphides* (not to be confused with the earlier work, though it has a similar mood to its second act). In 1937

Cats have always helped with paperwork

the company toured the 'watering places' of France with this production; at the first performance in Nice I had to fight my way through the difficult solo mazurka and, to my great relief, was promptly replaced. The role was far beyond my technique at that time – though I was given it again later when we were back in London.

There, in the tiny Mercury theatre, we learned and danced the works at the core of the classical ballet repertoire, in particular the choreography by Marius Petipa for the great Tchaikovsky ballets created in St Petersburg – *The Sleeping Beauty* and *Swan Lake*. My understanding and love of these works deepened during the Second World War, when I was engaged by Ninette de Valois to dance with the Sadler's Wells Ballet. With that company, amid the bombings and the desperate hopes and losses of these years, I had the good fortune to learn

*Giselle*, perhaps the greatest ballet of the French romantic tradition.

There are some who find its music banal; but I have heard viola players in hotel rooms across North America practising the second-act solo for hours on end. What counts always is not just the music on its own, but the total effect of a combination of music, design, scenario, choreography, interpretation, art, and conviction; and at that level *Giselle* is still a living challenge to dancers and an attraction to audiences after well over a hundred years of performances.

With Sadler's Wells I learned, too, the first and third acts of another classic, *Coppélia*. I was not dancing in the second act, and the scenery was so constructed that it blocked the view of the stage from any watching eyes and memories in the wings. But I learned it later, after I had joined the Metropolitan Ballet – a new company, started in London in 1947 by Mrs Cecilia

Blatch, of which I was ballet mistress. There I met Nicholas Beriozoff, who taught an excellent version of the second act. He also taught Michel Fokine's choreography for the *Polovtsian Dances* from Borodin's opera 'Prince Igor.' They were to make an exciting finale for the National Ballet's opening performance in 1951.

I had been lucky enough in England to learn the classical repertoire and experience the French and Russian traditions. We knew all about Diaghilev's productions in Paris in the early years of the century, and, from a visit by 'the Great Dane,' Erik Bruhn, to the Metropolitan Ballet, I knew something of the Danish tradition. But these were not the only works we danced: one-act ballets by English choreographers like Frederick Ashton, Antony Tudor, and Andrée Howard were also introduced to the public, and after the war we learned something of foreign contemporary choreo-

graphy through performances of visiting companies from the United States and France.

By the late forties, London was well on its way to becoming the ballet capital of the world. It had not had much of a tradition of its own to build on; many children of my generation had seen dance only at pierrot shows at the seaside. I did not see my first real ballet until about the age of twelve, when Colonel de Basil's Ballets Russes appeared at the Royal Opera House, Covent Garden. Although there had been excellent individual dancers in London in the earlier decades of the century, they had often appeared sandwiched between turns at music halls like the Alhambra. Male dancers were very rare. But the boom in entertainment during the Second World War had firmly established the Sadler's Wells Ballet, the Ballet Rambert, and others. Loyal audiences were built up, ready also to welcome foreign companies enthusiastically. And the London companies began to make overseas tours as well.

It was one such tour that was the indirect cause of a visit paid me in the late summer of 1950 when I was appearing in a mime play at the Mercury: a young man named Stewart James came with a rather vague proposal about a possible new ballet company in Canada.

I had never been to Canada, though if I had stayed with the Sadler's Wells Company I might have had the chance to go on the extremely successful tour it had made in 1949 of the United States and Canada. The United States had some professional ballet companies of its own, such as (despite its title) the Ballets Russes de Monte Carlo, Balanchine's New York City Ballet, and Ballet Theatre; but in Canada there was nothing comparable. A scattering of ballet schools offered the best they could and, in the circumstances, obviously could not aspire to a 'graduate' level of instruction.

Talented dancers, like Melissa Hayden, had been obliged to leave their native country to find professional training and career opportunities.

In such an environment, little wonder that the Sadler's Wells visit touched a sense of deprivation and sparked a longing for a Canadian professional company. Mrs F. J. Mulqueen, Mrs J. D. Woods, and Mrs R. B. Whitehead – three ladies of Toronto who had seen the Sadler's Wells performances and were interested in improving that city's cultural life – decided to do something about it. They approached the *grande dame* of ballet herself – Ninette de Valois, director of the Sadler's Wells Company. She advised them to try and form a national company which could draw its governors from all parts of Canada and which would hold nation-wide auditions to select its first dancers; this was the way to build up the widest possible interest and support, financial and otherwise. De Valois also recommended that they

A company sewing bee

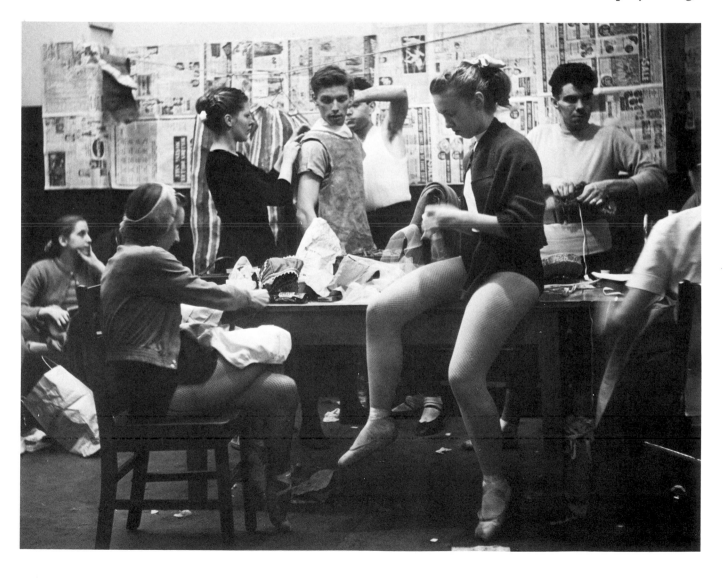

secure an experienced ballet person from outside Canada to set the artistic policy and to run the company.

It happened that a young Toronto balletomane who knew what the three ladies were thinking and what they had done was going to London on holiday that summer; he offered to scout around in search of a director. From the Royal Academy of Dancing he obtained a list of suitable candidates and took it to Ninette de Valois. She looked it over and said, 'Celia Franca, if you can get her.'

So it was that Stewart James came round to see me with this vague idea. There was, he explained, no organization, no money, no dancers; but possibly something might happen sometime.

Some weeks later, I received an invitation from the three Toronto ladies to fly over to Canada and see some performances in Montreal of the Ballet Festival Association. This organization gathered together semi-professional and amateur groups from across the country each year in a different city for a festival; the groups would show what they could do and try to arouse greater interest in the dance. By seeing their performances, I would be able to form an assessment of the dancing talent available in the country.

I agreed to come to the festival that November and found myself intrigued by the possibility that indeed a professional and national ballet company could be formed. I had to return to England, but I accepted an invitation to come back to Canada, where I had proposed to conduct an eight-month 'feasibility study' of such other questions as the existence of theatrical circuits. Such a study would allow me to make a much more informed assessment of the prospects for success.

In February 1951 I landed at Toronto airport, and my work in Canada began.

# Founding the Company

The T. Eaton Company, which had paid for my trip in November, had also agreed to support me while I conducted my research. A job was made for me on the top floor of their old College Street store in Toronto; as many will recall, that floor contained an auditorium and a restaurant called the Round Room. All that I had to do for Eaton's was some filing, a skill I had not hitherto possessed. I was free there, however, to meet all sorts of people who could enlighten me on the Canadian 'theatrical scene,' and often we would talk over long afternoon teas amid the gracious hats and murmur of the Round Room.

I remember Betty Oliphant coming to see me and the two of us sitting on a large oval pouffe in the foyer near the box office. Betty, later to become my ballet mistress and, more important, in 1959 principal of the National Ballet School, was representing the Canadian Dance Teachers Association. The teachers had heard rumours that I would draw dancers for the new company from only one school – the Boris Volkoff school in Toronto – and they were not unnaturally incensed. These were indeed but rumours, for it was policy to hold national auditions. Interest and even excitement were growing among the dancing schools about the new company, but I was not long in discovering that Canada was woefully short of suitable theatres and opera houses and that a theatrical circuit as such did not exist – as our first tours in a year or two were to make painfully yet at times hilariously evident.

Before I arrived in February, the three founding ladies – Sydney Mulqueen, Aileen Woods, and Pearl Whitehead – had prevailed upon three men to join them on a 'provisional' board of directors. They were Peter van Gelder, a former ambassador from the Netherlands; Robert A. Laidlaw, a well-known Toronto philan-thropist who was a patron of the

Lilian Jarvis in the St Lawrence Hall;
the 'facilities' were behind the screen

Hospital for Sick Children, Upper Canada College, the McMichael Art Gallery at Kleinburg, and later of the National Ballet and its School; and Walter L. Gordon. Walter was then a leading Toronto accountant and business consultant, unaware that he was destined to become a controversial minister of finance at Ottawa during the sixties. He was very cautious in 1951, however, for when the board decided in April that year that they should establish a permanent board and try to plunge ahead, he withdrew, though he gave us a most helpful donation.

He retained his interest in us. Later, when he was chancellor of York University, he conferred on me an honorary degree. My ceremony was in the morning, and in the afternoon John Kenneth Galbraith was to receive an LLD; we both replied to toasts at the luncheon. Since another economist, John Maynard Keynes, had married a famous Diaghilev ballerina, Lydia Lopokova, there was

something on which to pin a speech for such a daunting occasion.

Our first and beloved president of the board was Z.R.B. (Bobs) Lash. He looked after our incorporation and the establishment of the permanent board. It was called the National Ballet Guild of Canada and served as the governing body of the actual company, which started life under the title of the Canadian National Ballet. As time went on, these names began to seem clumsy and confusing. The Canadian National Ballet 'sounds like the railway,' said a new director, Mrs George Hees (Mabel or Mibs, as she was called by her friends); so it was changed to the present title. And in the seventies the word 'Guild' was dropped so that the governing body is now known simply as the board of directors of the National Ballet of Canada.

Mabel Hees had been asked to join the board by Aileen Woods. 'There won't be much to do,' said

Aileen, since Mibs was already active on behalf of the Toronto Symphony Orchestra. She became a pillar of strength to us, as on one special occasion did her husband.

In March 1954, during our first tour of the United States, the company found itself stranded in Seattle, with no money to get home. Mibs could not sleep. George refused to let her lose her sleep over the ballet, so he went down to the National Trust and ordered $20 000 sent to the company that day.

    'And what will the security be?'
    'No security.'
    'And the rate of interest?'
    'No interest.'
    'That's not very business-like.'
    'Right. Send it.'
We paid back every cent.

Such generosity and confidence was very heartening, though it occurred some three years after the founding year of 1951 and by then there was indeed something to show. To start with, the guild, studded though it was with emi-nent Toronto businessmen or their wives, had very little money, and it proceeded with infinite financial caution. There were board meet-ings every two weeks of that spring, and its membership was rather flexible for a while. Although Walter Gordon and Robert Laidlaw formally left the board, they nevertheless showed up at the next meeting, bringing with them E.W. Bickle, a mining magnate. George Craig, Norman Seagram and Bradford Heintzman appeared at our eighth meeting; Edwin Goodman and Arthur Gelber, with 'Jack Allen as an interested onlooker' were present at the ninth. Jack Allen and Martin Baldwin, curator of the Art Gallery of Ontario, were appointed to the board as of September. Joseph Whitmore, former president of the Ballet Festival Association, was another interested board member.

By the end of the summer, the board and its 'interested patrons' comprised a strong, representative, and influential group of men and women. We were fortunate in having such a group of people as our shield and sponsors; but they were tough-minded, as perhaps lawyers and accountants and businessmen ought to be, and it largely fell to me to show them that their venture of supporting a ballet company could prove a success.

Although the provisional board had agreed in April that it should become a permanent board, its members were not going to commit themselves to the launching of a ballet company until about the end of my eight months of study and research. While the board was considering the potential financial resources available and required, I felt the need to spur them on by proving that Canadian talent and audiences existed.

I therefore accepted an offer to produce a *ballet concert* as part of the Promenade concert series then held during the summer in the university hockey arena. Our group of twelve dancers, sensing the urgency of the project, rehearsed long hours into the night without remuneration. The fee I received just covered expenses; my board was relieved not to be financially involved and at the same time pleased that we were well received by the critics.

As a result of this little triumph, I was invited to present a similar concert at the Chalet de la Montagne in Montreal in August. Mme Antonia David would pay me $900 after the performance, but I was able to borrow the money from the guild to pay the travelling and other expenses of the little troupe I took to Montreal. This production – of the second act of *Coppélia* – was also well received, and just broke even financially.

My second project was to try and establish a summer school for teachers and students. This I considered of the utmost importance. Students could not develop to their fullest if there were not well-trained teachers to guide them; and the students themselves, having sampled good training, would demand a higher standard of instruction from their teachers. If we were ever to have professional Canadian ballet, we had to improve its teaching.

Many Canadian teachers of those years would spend time and their hard-earned dollars at summer 'dance conventions' in the United States; they joined hundreds of American dance teachers on the slippery floors of hotel ballrooms to learn ballet variations, tap routines, recital numbers, and what have you. At the end, they would perhaps receive a pattern for a recital costume, some mimeographed music, notes on the dances they had learned, and a diploma to hang on their studio walls. What they were not taught was *how* to teach, and they received little exposure to the finer points and higher techniques of ballet dancing. An annual summer school would change that and in the process develop the larger pool of talent which a national com-

pany would require.

The board was nervous. Nevertheless, Pearl Whitehead and I, at Stewart James' suggestion, arranged with the Board of Control of the City of Toronto to rent the St Lawrence Hall for a nominal fee and have it painted and put in some order. Following my request to the board for a loan of $400 to send out notices and press releases about the school, the board agreed, but with the following stipulations:

1/ School to be conducted by Miss Franca under sponsorship of National Ballet Guild – with no financial responsibility to the Board of Directors – profit or loss to be for Miss Franca's personal account.
2/ Guild has advanced sum of $400 to defray initial expenses and is to be repaid from profits of the school.
3/ Guild indemnified City against damages to St Lawrence Hall – other than fire – Miss

Franca to take out adequate insurance.

4/ If school shows profit – Miss Franca will use such to travel to West Coast and intervening cities for the purpose of auditioning dancers for the Canadian National Ballet Company, if and when formed.

Happily, the summer school was also a financial success, and I promptly paid back the $400. The board, encouraged by the reception given these ventures, decided towards the end of August that it would indeed found a ballet company. The days of tentative and conditional moves were largely over. The commitment had been made, and the formation of the company was announced to the world.

With the profits of the summer school and a generous donation from the Canadian Dance Teachers Association, I flew off on my auditioning trip to the cities of western Canada. Stewart James came with me, and I invited the successful candidates to come to Toronto to begin rehearsals in mid-September.

# Our First Performance

The St Lawrence Hall, still attached to a farmers' market, was not in those days one of the amenities of the city of Toronto. It certainly had character, but the roof leaked and there was no heating supplied until later in the year. Even then, it was inadequate: while the radiators vocalized loudly, they didn't produce much heat. We would sometimes exercise in our overcoats, and at one desperate point the dancers threatened to strike. Our lease expired in the late autumn, since the building was used as a hostel for the indigent during the winter.

For dancers, however, it had one rare advantage – a floor of real *unwaxed* wood. Many times in the future we would have to turn down engagements because we were offered a stage floor built on concrete; dancers need the resilience of a wooden floor, for too often have muscles been strained or spines jarred in dancing on floors that did not have enough 'give.'

We borrowed a large rectangular mirror so that the dancers could watch themselves during rehearsals. Unfortunately we couldn't place the mirror upright but had to lean it on its long side against the small platform that masqueraded as a stage at the end of our bare rehearsal room. If one stood close to the platform, all one could see were legs and feet; a few feet away, one could see one's whole body but only by looking down. For some years we had the most down-cast-eyed company of dancers in the world.

There were twenty-nine of us. In accordance with our national purpose, the dancers I found came from as many provinces as possible at that time. We were nineteen girls and ten boys.

The only Canadian dancer I had known before coming to Canada was David Adams. He had danced with the Winnipeg Ballet before coming to England to work with the Sadler's Wells and then the Metropolitan Ballet; there we had sometimes danced together in Victor

A group around the *barre*

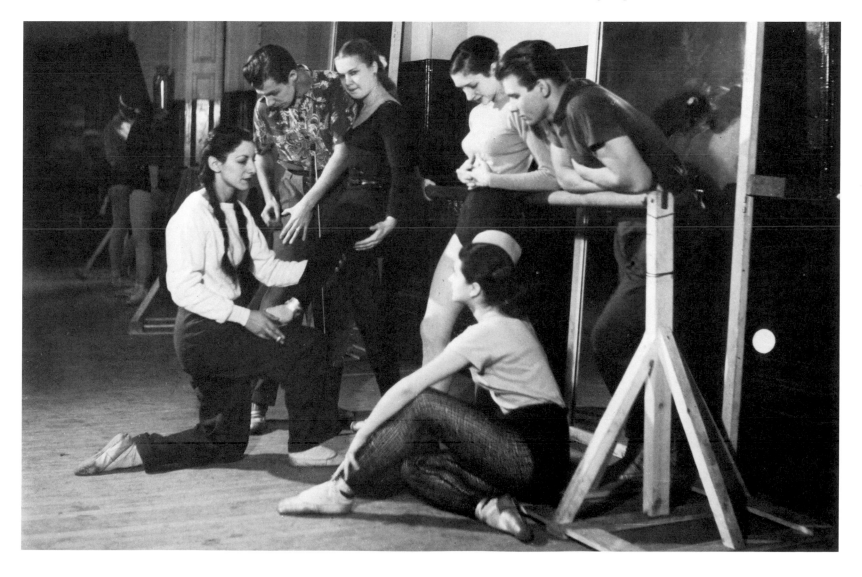

Gsovsky's *The Dances of Galanta*. In the late forties, he returned to Vancouver where, fortunately for me and the National Ballet, he met and married Lois Smith.

Lois had had ballet training, but had never danced in a professional ballet company; nevertheless, with her beautiful legs and feet, natural classical line, and zeal she was destined to become our first principal ballerina. David was an excellent partner for her: Lois, though on the tall side, had a delicate, fragile appearance; David was built like a football player, and his muscular physique showed off Lois' femininity to advantage.

Our other principal dancers were another married team, Irene Apiné and Jury Gotshalks. Latvian by birth, they had settled in Halifax after the war and taught there until the National Ballet was formed. Their dance technique – particularly Irene's – was quite strong, and they had considerable theatrical experience in Europe – an asset in a group which was then semi-

amateur. Irene and Jury stayed with the company for four years. Their style of dancing could be unabashedly acrobatic. In their pas de deux from *Don Quixote*, for example, they would like the music to be slowed down and held while they displayed a one-handed lift; our conductor, George Crum, would then, with my complicity, do his crafty best to 'accidentally on purpose' keep the tempo moving.

But the Gotshalks were experienced, and that was important. Most of the dancers during that first season were amateurs, being paid starvation wages and being forced by me to behave, and to *want* to behave, as professionals. That, at least, is what many of them now tell me.

One pretty girl who felt the serious destiny of these rehearsals and who – no wonder – was also Ken Bell's favourite photographic model was Judie Colpman. Those big brown eyes, the luxurious chestnut-brown hair, and the dimples! She had, as a child, been taken to the Eaton auditorium, and the prospect of actually performing there herself filled her with wonderment. She says she was nervous but happy, though she had terrible trouble arranging her hair in the classical style for *Les Sylphides.* She remembers the affection the dancers all held for each other and the fine team spirit of the company. In the following season, I gave Judie her first leading role as the Milkmaid in *Le Pommier,* and she later progressed to the Bluebird pas de deux in a divertissement version of *Sleeping Beauty* and to Swanilda in *Coppélia.*

Among our number then was the versatile Lilian Jarvis. When she had auditioned for me at Mildred Wikson's studio in Toronto, I found her classical technique rather weak, but her soft expressive arms won me over. In the prelude of *Les Sylphides,* her lyrical quality was fully evident. I further exploited it by choreographing a new version of *L'Après-midi d'un faune* to Debussy's music with Lilian dancing the principal nymph to Grant Strate's faun. Her feminine vulnerability when startled by the faun was stressed by her frankly sensuous delight as she 'bathed' with the other nymphs. Shc was as delectable in soubrette roles such as Pineapple Poll in John Cranko's ballet and Swanilda in *Coppélia.*

Grant Strate was a dancer with virtually no training in classical ballet, but he looked as if he might develop – and from the beginning I was intent on developing the individual talents of our dancers – into a good mime-dancer. His first performance was as Jokanaan, a prophet similar to John the Baptist in the Bible, whose head is cut off in *The Dance of Salome;* his later acting roles included an old man in *Le Pommier,* Dr Coppélius in *Coppélia,* and the Duke of Verona and Friar Laurence in *Romeo and Juliet.* He also developed into a choreographer, and often cast Lilian Jarvis in his ballets, most notably as the Mermaid in *The Fisherman and His Soul* and as the Young Girl in *Ballad.*

Another talent in the company then was Angela Leigh, although she had no solo work at first. She began to show promise, as a leading Wili in the second act of *Giselle* and as a Fairy in the second act of the *Nutcracker.* She also showed technical promise in David Adams' *Ballet Composite,* choreographed to Brahms' 'Variations on a Theme of Haydn.' But after Angela's delicate and subtle performance as Camargo in *Ballet behind Us,* a satirical history of dance, I was convinced that her forte was her piquant sense of humour. No matter how serious her future roles – Odette-Odile in *Swan Lake,* Barbara Allen, or the Witch in *The Fisherman and His Soul,* among many – a smile insisted on squeezing itself out of me. I loved Angela in her witty representations in Ashton's *Les Rendez-vous,* in Ray Powell's *One in Five,* Adams' *Pas de chance,*

and, although she disliked the role, as the Nurse in *Romeo and Juliet* – one of the best interpretations we have had. She also excelled as the Russian ballerina in Tudor's *Gala Performance* and as the Queen of the Carriage Trade in his *Offenbach in the Underworld.*

The twenty-nine of us had a hectic time rehearsing in the old St Lawrence Hall. Each morning we would begin with a class for an hour and a half, and then rehearsals continued relentlessly during the rest of the day. When dancers had a short break, they would climb up the rickety staircase to the balcony, where they would flake out in the accumulated dust and pigeon-droppings.

The pigeons were a feature recalled by all the dancers I have talked to recently about these early days: they nested inside the building on cornices under the ceiling and would occasionally fly down over the dancers, apparently to check what was going on. The balcony itself was considered

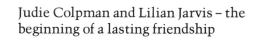

Judie Colpman and Lilian Jarvis – the beginning of a lasting friendship

Ups and downs

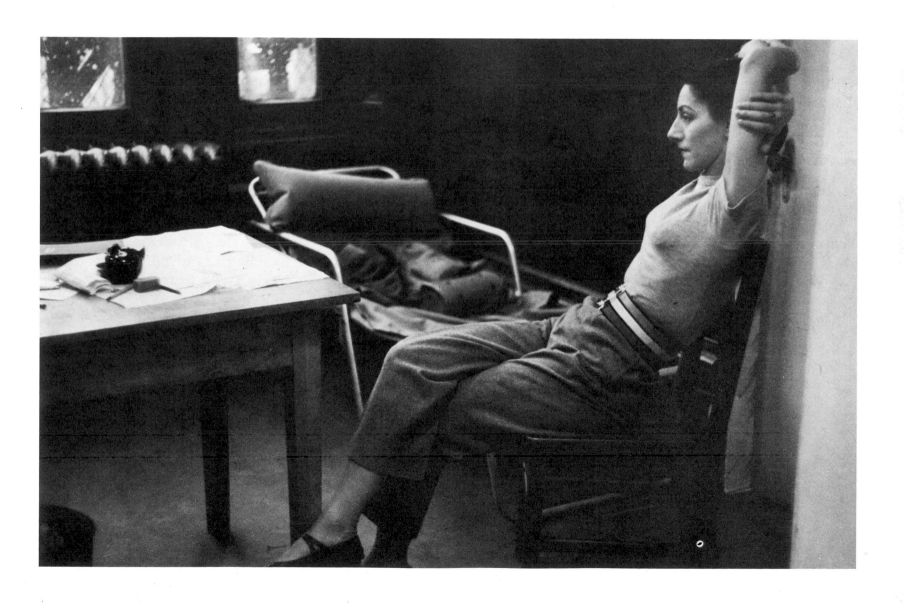

Pearl Whitehead in 1978

structurally unsound, and eventually, haunted by the prospect of its collapsing with some of the company among the ruins, I forbade the dancers' going up there.

The dressing rooms were makeshift, the toilets primitive, and the showers, if drops of tepid water dribbling from a showerhead could be called showers, were in a room whose floor and rusted gratings would impress anyone as a natural home for the viruses that cause athlete's foot and plantar warts. Each evening, as we flopped exhausted down to the street to go home, we could see rats among the heaps of garbage from the market at the bottom of the stairs.

In the midst of this squalor, there occurred one bright spot: the directors treated the company, about two weeks before the end of rehearsals, to a lunch there of oysters and beer. Our rehearsal afterwards, of *Salome,* was taking us nowhere, so we all went home early that day.

Besides practising, the dancers

had to help in the making of their own costumes. We were making properties in the St Lawrence Hall too, and in off-moments or at the end of the day or at their homes at night the dancers had to sew on buttons and sequins. The company's first wardrobe mistress cum chief cutter was Celia Sutton, a lovely redhead and former beautician at Eaton's with whom I had become friendly while stationed there to make my survey. We often took our coffee breaks together, and thus I discovered her interest in dress-making.

By this time too, thanks to the initiative of Pearl Whitehead, George Crum had met our company. His contribution to its development over the years has been too much taken for granted. Besides conducting the orchestra, scanty and deprived though it was for many years, he arranged scores for us, he played one of the two pianos we used in the early tours when we couldn't afford an orchestra at all, he suggested

Note the long mirror, borrowed from
Eaton's and placed against the stage

Canadian composers to our choreographers (and then handled the business arrangements). And he buoyed up our spirits, keeping us amused, and sometimes exasperated, by his constant stream of stories , both clean and dirty. He continues in most of these duties and activities, with our gratitude.

In the summer of 1951, Pearl Whitehead had taken the plunge and booked the Eaton auditorium for nine performances in all – three in November, three in January 1952, and three in April. She was, and remains, the most positive person I have ever met; when one remembers that our organization was almost penniless, her action required courage. I believe that she went ahead and booked the auditorium without as much as a by-your-leave from the other directors; doubtless she knew that procrastination and uncertainty would get us nowhere. She simply came to me one day and said 'I've done it!'

I had to decide on a program

for these performances. For November, *Les Sylphides* seemed a good opening item, lyrical and an established part of the classical repertoire. For drama, we had *The Dance of Salome,* which I had adapted for a BBC television version made in 1949. Based on the play 'Salome' by Oscar Wilde, it was the first ballet commissioned specially for television. James Hartley, then head of the BBC TV music department, had composed the score, which had been orchestrated by a commercial firm. I gave the full score to George Crum, who in turn gave it to Oskar Morawetz, the well-known Canadian composer, to reduce it for the small orchestra of nineteen players to be hired for our Eaton auditorium performances. There were copyists' mistakes in the parts, and my hair started to go grey over the time taken to sort them out and correct them. We could afford but six hours' rehearsal time with the orchestra for the whole program. But in one

Artists of the ballet at a rehearsal for our
first production of *Les Sylphides*

matter, our transcription saved money: Hartley had written the music for the sensuous Dance of the Seven Veils in 3/4 time but with an accent on every fourth beat. Our version was simply put into 4/4 time, which of course sounded exactly the same and was much easier for the musicians to read and master.

Then, for something cheerful, we had Lois Smith and David Adams dancing the peasant pas de deux from *Giselle* – an item they had performed earlier at the second Varsity Arena Promenade concert which had taken place by special request on 13 September. For something created by a Canadian, I asked Kay Armstrong to come from Vancouver and rehearse her *Etude* to the June Barcarolle from Tchaikovsky's 'Seasons.' This pleasing abstract piece was danced by Earl Kraul, later to become a principal and replace David Adams as Lois Smith's main partner, and by three long-legged ladies, Maria Dynowska, Natalia Butko, and

Katherine Stewart.

For the final number on our opening program, I chose the *Polovtsian Dances* from 'Prince Igor.' This was a very conscious choice on my part, since there was in 1951 a strong prejudice against male dancers among Canadian men. We had to affect a 'butch' image. Our early audiences were largely female, and our committee ladies and our own educational and promotional efforts strove to dispel this prejudiced conception of ballet. Fortunately, the men on our committees were also all in favour of the company and worked to entice others into the theatres.

Well, in these virile and pagan Russian dances, our boys gave their all! The energy they expended and the dust they raised, beating their bows on the ground and throwing them in the air! You should have seen them raping the slave girls: their actions were so realistic at times that I had to bring myself, in the name of art, to restrain their enthusiasm. Besides,

Opening night! Margaret Skinner, Angela Labatt, and Alan Skinner

the girls were getting bruised. And black and blue marks on the arms could show through the liquid white body make-up used in the poetic *Les Sylphides*.

One night during a later performance of the *Dances*, I stood in the wings to watch. Myrna Aaron was troubled by poor eyesight and, contact lenses not then being common and beautiful oriental slave girls not being allowed to wear spectacles on stage, she was felled in a particularly lively encounter with a warrior. She crawled on her hands and knees off to the wings. As I helped her up, she said, 'Christ, I hope Franca didn't see that.'

We rehearsed on the stage of the Eaton auditorium one or two days before our début on 12 November 1951. A perfectly respectable backdrop depicting moonlit ruins had been designed by James Pape, but when it was first hung I could not believe my eyes: the scene painters had covered everything with snow! When I asked about

this, I was told that 'it would make it more Canadian.' The lighting was organized at the last minute, however. In fact, while I was putting on my make-up on opening night, the stage manager rushed into my room to ask what colour gelatins to use for the third pipe or some such thing. All I could think of was how to hide that wretched backdrop: I believe we smothered it in 32 blue – the darkest possible.

My dressing room was a lively place that night. One girl was having trouble putting on lipstick; another's feet had swollen and she could not get into her pointe shoes; someone had a 'blank' and could not remember the choreography. Kay Ambrose never had time to take the cigarette out of her mouth except to light a fresh one. She flitted from room to room, helping dancers with their hair styles and make-up.

The dancers had had no rehearsal with the orchestra, but most of them were too inexperienced

The first of many bouquets for Lois Smith

to realize how dangerous this was. Fortunately also, they did not understand the awful implications latent in such happenings as a different electrician turning up for the show from the one who was at the rehearsal. There were indeed some technical hitches to the first performance, but the general effect was good, and the audience applauded each ballet warmly. The dancers pulled together marvelously and truly looked as though they had worked as a company for months rather than weeks. Over the three-night engagement, more than 90 per cent of the seats were sold, and our souvenir programs were eagerly picked up. All told, it was a good beginning.

After the curtain calls on the first night, George Craig, one of our directors, was to come on stage and make a speech. We had usually seen him earlier, seated on any old dirty chair behind any old dirty table, handing out to the dancers their meagre weekly pay. That night, he came backstage in his dinner jacket, accompanied by Sydney Mulqueen, and waited in the wings, more nervous than the dancers. She steadied his nerves with two miniature bottles of cognac, and his speech was fine.

The board of directors held a reception for the company after that first performance. I now remember little about it, except the sinister presence of Lady Tupper, who had been invited to represent the Winnipeg Ballet Company. She had previously referred to us as the 'Toronto upstarts.'

# The First Year

After our début the company resumed rehearsals and proceeded to enlarge its repertoire. In keeping with our resources, we had to start with acts or scenes from long works or with shorter modern works. For our three nights in January 1952 we produced the second act of *Giselle,* David Adams' *Ballet Composite,* and the second act of *The Nutcracker;* and in March we presented *Etude,* our new *L'Après-midi d'un faune,* Adams' new *Ballet behind Us* (with costumes by Suzanne Mess, who was to become one of North America's most important opera designers), and a repeat of the act from *The Nutcracker.*

I remember the first performance which the National Ballet was *invited* to give. The 'village' of Forest Hill in Toronto agreed to pay $500 for a performance in order 'to encourage the company.' We were duly grateful (though it turned out that we lost money on the engagement), and on the evening of 10 December, we trooped up to the auditorium in Forest Hill Collegiate; the stage was tiny – it felt no bigger than fifteen feet square – but we managed to squeeze onto it *Les Sylphides,* the pas de deux from *Giselle,* the *Don Quixote* pas de deux, *Etude,* and the second act of *Coppélia.* After dancing our hearts out and trying very hard to please, we were treated to a reception of coffee and sandwiches made from rather old white bread. Our stomachs were growling, and we longed for hot food. A clot from the audience approached me and said, 'Hardly Sadler's Wells!' In a paroxysm of self-control, I smiled benignly at him, as I have done countless times since at other patronising simpletons, in the belief that he could become in the future a regular attender at our performances. He did.

We also received an invitation to perform at the Toronto Police Association's annual concert in February. This was an occasion of a completely different kind: it took place in the Maple Leaf Gardens, a

Jury Gotshalks prepares to be the Polovtsian chief

vast hockey arena with appalling acoustics and sight lines, despite all of which the Metropolitan Opera, the Red Army Chorus, the Royal and Kirov ballet companies, and many other large attractions have in their day filled the thousands of seats. The program was as popular as could be: the Toronto Symphony Orchestra played Berlioz' Roman Carnival overture, a baritone sang 'None but the Lonely Heart,' and we put on our two most exuberant productions – the pas de deux from *Don Quixote* and, of course, our *Polovtsian Dances*. This was not a time for finesse, polish, sophistication, or understatement – these finer points were to come later.

This may be time to recall another enterprise we engaged in, later that year, where 'mass entertainment' was called for.

The grounds of the Canadian National Exhibition in Toronto lie beside Lake Ontario and contain a grandstand. It is a tradition that a 'show' be performed in it for the three weeks of the CNE. In 1952, as perhaps one of the signals of a growing Canadian nationalism, it was agreed that the show would be run by Canadians instead of Americans, as had been the practice in the past. Jack Arthur, known in Canada as 'Mr Showbusiness,' was commissioned to produce the Grandstand Show, and our company was invited to perform in the middle of the program. There was a slick chorus line, 'The Canadettes,' choreographed by Jack Arthur's wife, Midge; Alan and Blanche Lund did some of their fabulous duets in the Astaire-Rogers style; Eric Christmas was an excellent comedian; the Leslie Bell Singers sang; Max Ferguson gave us one of his 'Rawhide' sketches; Tony Martin was the headliner, and a good pro who managed to project his voice and personality across to the audience sitting almost a quarter of a mile away.

And there were we, in the middle of a field on a enormous stage (for once). The wind and the

The chief in action

A famous partnership begins – Lois Smith and David Adams

Sunlight hits David in the St Lawrence
Hall

rain blew in like furies from the lake. We were trying to perform a fantasy I had choreographed to Mendelssohn's incidental music to 'A Midsummer Night's Dream.'

Our small band of dancers had been augmented for the occasion, and Kay was designing the costumes; but because of various blow-ups with unions she ended up as Jack's assistant, practically designing the whole show. In the ballet there was almost everything I could think of in nature: bees; an enormous rotten apple out of which crawled dancing caterpillars; fairies, of course; mushrooms eighteen feet high; and in the middle of the performance I manoeuvred the dancers into the shape of a butterfly. At a lighting rehearsal Jack Arthur exclaimed, 'She's given me a butterfly. Now I gotta light it.'

I hadn't wanted to call this production *Midsummer Night's Dream*, but Jack had insisted on it, since the public, he said, would be attracted by a title they had heard

of. The ballet did not follow Shakespeare's plot at all, though Lois Smith and David Adams could have been Titania and Oberon in their pas de deux. Lois was the only dancer apart from myself I dared put *sur la pointe*, but she found it very difficult to keep her balance when the gales came sweeping in.

I made a grand entrance, rather à la Queen of the Night, coming down a long staircase to the stage seated upon the shoulders of Earl Kraul and Bob van Norman; attached to my shoulders was a long train of turquoise blue chiffon, the ends of which were held by two fairy attendants. As I descended, it unfurled in the breezes and created, so I thought, an eye-catching and novel effect. But the whole operation was dangerous. I remember putting the fear of God into my *porteurs* at the dress rehearsal by yelling 'If you drop me, I'll kill you!'

Such refinement!

In January 1952 we had made our

first out-of-town tour, to Guelph, Kitchener, Montreal, London, and Hamilton, all one-night stands except for four nights at His Majesty's theatre in Montreal and three nights at the Grand theatre in London. At least in Montreal and London there were humble but legitimate theatres; it was the visits to smaller towns to give a single performance in a school auditorium that made us realize what we were really up against as far as facilities were concerned. We were a national company, and touring was, as it still is, an important part of the National Ballet's operations.

It was especially important to tour during the company's fledgling years, since we had to show the Canadian public that we in fact existed. We could not generate enough press or radio attention across the country by simply exercising in a Toronto rehearsal room; we could not expect any support, whether by government grants or by attendance or dona-tions, from a public which had no opportunity to see us.

Besides, without a national audience there would be no chance for the company to develop. There were not enough performing opportunities for the dancers in Toronto alone, and there was not the audience to fill a theatre for even a short season. So tours we had to make, even though my survey had shown that no theatrical circuit existed. That we managed to perform across Canada in 1952 was a tremendous achievement – though it was an effort no one in their right mind would have attempted. But we were young, enthusiastic, adventurous. Off we went into the theatrical wilderness.

Our small company gathered for its first tour 'under the clock' at Union Station in Toronto to catch a train to Guelph. We had, of course, no orchestra travelling with us, and George Crum had made special musical arrangements for two pianos – one of which he would play himself – of the works we needed where we weren't going to hire a local orchestra.

Under the clock, our other pianist took fright for some reason and fled. We could manage the warm-up class without a piano (George never would, could, or did play for class); it wouldn't have been the first time I had counted out the rhythms I taught. But what of the performance that night in the High School auditorium? We were lucky – we found a good pianist in Guelph who virtually sightread the second piano part. That problem overcome, we then hit another.

The auditorium was dismal: the stage was no more than a small platform; there were no flies; there was hardly any lighting equipment. I had wanted to purchase some lighting for tours, but rental was cheaper, and we had some in our baggage. But it was inadequate – the performance was well-nigh invisible. And there was no way one could imagine that the gloom was an intended artistic effect.

(By comparison, the company now uses a 45-foot truck, containing 30 000 pounds of computerized lighting gear, to take on its North American tours. This cost $200 000, paid for with the help of grants from the Kresge Foundation and the Ontario lottery.)

Taking our baggage by train was always a problem. We hired a small truck in Toronto which could carry some scenery cut-outs, a second-hand and faded skycloth, and a few hampers of costumes and properties. These items were driven to Union Station and loaded into a baggage car of the train, in which they could travel free as long as we bought a certain number of passenger tickets. At our destination we would first have to hire another truck to move the things to the theatre, and then another to deliver them all back to the depot for the next train we had to catch. The stage management staff would anxiously watch the clock towards

*Giselle* at the Royal Alex, with Celia Franca as Giselle and David Adams as Albrecht

The final scene from Act I of *Giselle* (left), and the Wilis in Act II, with Lois Smith as their Queen

the end of the performance, worrying if all the baggage could be packed and taken to the station before the train's departure time.

The worst thing about travelling by train on tight one-night-stand schedules was the habit of the railway companies of shunting the baggage car off to a distant siding as soon as the train arrived at its destination; we would then spend hours, intended to be devoted to setting up the stage and so on, looking for the baggage car and then going through the loading and unloading routine. There were even occasions when the train would stop before our destination and the baggage car would be removed and left there, while the National Ballet members travelled on in blissful ignorance...

One aspect of our organization had developed, however, by the time we made this first tour: a branch of the National Ballet Guild had been founded in London on 31 December 1951, and we were for-tunate in recruiting Mrs Hugh (Angela) Labatt and Dr Alan Skinner (long a ballet enthusiast) to the national board. The branch had fifty-eight members by the end of 1952, and their fees and dona-tions were welcome additions to our coffers.

The national board of the guild was very aware that its national company ought to appear in the province of Quebec as soon as possible. Mabel Hees, our new general manager Walter Hom-burger and I had gone to Montreal to talk with interested people at the Art Gallery in December 1951. This helped towards the founding of a branch there on 3 January 1952, with Mrs Keith (Millie) Hutchison as president. She was a strong leader who gathered round many energetic and capable workers. Jack Eaton offered to sponsor the first night of our performances in Montreal; the Montreal Dance Teachers Association sponsored a matinée for children; some organi-zations might be expected to

Franca and Adams at the end of the Adagio in *Giselle.* Below, Robert Hall's set for *Dance of Salome*

Jury Gotshalks and Irene Apiné hold it in the studio for a photograph of their pas de deux from *Don Quixote*

purchase blocks of tickets for other performances. Thus we tried to ensure respectable audiences and continuing support in that city.

The part played by Walter Homburger in the company was another welcome improvement. He it was who had booked and arranged our first tour. Edwin Goodman and Arthur Gelber on the national board had sought out and obtained his services on a so-called part-time basis as our general manager. Walter's main work was directing the International Artists Concert Agency which he had established in 1947 to bring world-renowned artists to perform in Toronto. For a small fee, we now had the benefit of his services and those of his secretary – no small advantage to a company that did not even have an office or a phone.

For our four nights in Montreal and our three in London, I was able to vary the program for each performance. We had added *The Dance of Salome,* the second act of *Giselle,* and *Ballet Composite* to the touring repertoire and so hoped to entice people to come to more than one performance. This was hard on our small stage crew, who now had more lighting plots to adjust and scenery to move around more often.

Our début in Montreal seems to have been a success; the first night was sold out, and the papers said it 'was quite a revelation.' 'Montreal was invaded last night – and succumbed without a struggle.' It was even controversial, for some Jewish members of the audience objected to my treatment of the Jewish characters in *Salome* and asked Arthur Gelber to have them removed from the ballet. I refused, in that they were an integral part of Wilde's play, on which the ballet was based. Though it made balanced programming difficult, *Salome* being the only contemporary dramatic work we had at that time, I chose to remove it from the repertoire after our first year.

In Montreal, as in London, we

Scenes from Acts I and III of the first
full-length *Coppélia.* It was the company's
most popular production until *The
Nutcracker* of 1964-65. Lois Smith is
Swanilda and David Adams is Franz

had decided that the occasion merited the hiring of an orchestra. George Crum went there ahead of time to rehearse with the orchestra a local concertmaster had brought together. He arrived at His Majesty's theatre to discover the concertmaster rehearsing his group in Vivaldi's 'Four Seasons' for a visit by the Winnipeg Ballet (which had cleverly booked the theatre a few days ahead of us!). The level of playing for our performance was not what it should have been. But at least, on *this* occasion, George did not have to sing.

When we arrived next in London, we found that the orchestra retained for us there had a student as concertmaster, a fourteen-year-old flutist, and several members to whom George Crum had to teach the rudimentary qualities and techniques of their instruments. There was very little time or money for rehearsal. We were going to perform the second act of *Coppélia* and intended playing the famous waltz from the first act as an overture. At the rehearsal, George, conducting with one beat to the bar, was interrupted by the concertmaster, who declared that the work was A WALTZ. It eventually dawned on George that the concertmaster presumed that, since a waltz was written in 3/4 time, it ought properly to be conducted with three clear beats to the bar. In the performance of *Les Sylphides*, where the first solo is danced to a brilliant Chopin waltz in G flat major, the melody is carried by the flute: it is fast, exposed, wide-ranging, in a tricky key. The less said about this performance the better. The melody also disappeared in the faster parts of the *Polovtsian Dances* when the violins just failed to come in. This time George had no choice but to sing out 'diddily, diddily, diddily, diddily, diddily, diddily,' etc., in his croaking voice in an attempt to keep everyone together.

The audience loved it. They were splitting their sides laughing,

Over, Lilian Jarvis and Grant Strate (centre) in the opening scene of *L'Apres-midi d'un faune*

particularly when George's hoarse voice broke in upon the frantic pandemonium. The dancers, struggling amid the barely recognizable music, dared not take their eyes off the conductor for fear of losing their bearings and bumping into one another. Many people who came on the first night came again to enjoy these great moments in the history of ballet.

But good-natured hilarity prevailed over any professional sense of horror. We made staunch friends in London as a result of these performances; Londoners billeted the dancers and fed them; volunteers brought coffee and home-made goodies and set up a cafeteria under the stage. This style of warm hospitality, imitated later by the Windsor branch of the guild, had its disadvantages too, however. It might save the company the costs of bed and board, but some dancers forgot their diet and stuffed themselves on sweet and fattening foods, with no benefit to their health, their appearance on stage,

or their bursting costumes.

Montreal had showered us with hospitality too a week or so before, when the mayor, Camillien Houde, held an official reception in the Windsor Hotel for the company after the premiere. Here too, in my view, some of our dancers had not been on their best behaviour. There was a dance band at the reception, and a few couples could not be separated from that dance floor; when the band was supposed to go home, the mayor felt obliged to rehire it to keep the dancers happy. He himself and his wife soon left, exhausted, while the high spirits continued on the dance floor. Determined that we should never outstay our welcome again, I made a practice of wandering around receptions after that whispering with a fixed and determined smile. 'Time to go home now...'

We made two other trips out of Toronto in our first year – to the Palace theatre in St Catharines and

the Savoy theatre in Hamilton. We felt most encouraged by the reception we received there, as elsewhere during our first season, and the dancers were enthusiastic and eager to continue. The twenty-two performances had served to whet their appetites, even though their salaries had been cut by five dollars a week in the middle of January.

The first annual meeting of the National Ballet Guild took place in June 1952. The treasurer reported a shameful deficit on the first year's operations of $24.18, but he was relieved to declare that it had since been covered. The directors were not too disappointed or anxious. The chairman, Norman Seagram, said 'the National Ballet Company of Canada was the fulfilment of a hope...' In the management committee's report, Edwin Goodman 'paid tribute to the foresight and courage of the original group of men and women...who had launched the venture' and also 'expressed unbounded confidence

in the Artistic Director of the National Ballet Company and forecast its successful future.'

In my report, I summarized the performances of the season and then explained my long-term policy for the company. I wished to 'establish gradually a good representation of classical ballets because they set a standard for both artists and public. I would like to think of our National Ballet developing and maturing year after year until it becomes part of Canadian life.' I wished further to introduce '*at least* one or two new ballets each year to be choreographed by Canadians. Without new works any form of art will stagnate.' But I also hoped 'to employ the services of guest choreographers at such time *a)* when the company has matured and is ready to absorb new styles; *b)* when the company and its repertoire is in need of an outside stimulus.'

I must have had some premonitions in writing that report for I also said: 'There has never been a

After applause for her performance as
Giselle, Celia Franca had then to appeal to
the audience for funds to help keep the
company going . . .

ballet company in existence which has not been left by dancers in search of more remunerative engagements, and inevitably amongst their number are dancers whose value has been built up by the very company they are leaving. The history of ballet is well scarred by the antics of such principals, who often return to their original nests after various experiences in the outside world. But those dancers who have the integrity and vision to withstand tempting offers from those impermanent and attractive concerns which periodically materialize are those who will personally reap the reward of an entire company's artistic success. That is why, when assessing a dancer's work, one must look for integrity and honesty as well as technical proficiency.'

I also pointed out that ballet is 'more easily appreciated when the performance takes place in a large and well-equipped theatre.' If I longed for such theatres at the end of our first year, my longing was immeasurably deeper and more poignant when we returned from our main endeavour in the autumn of 1952 – a tour of western Canada.

*A Western Tour*

For a poor touring ballet company in 1952, the West was still wild. We knew there was no theatrical circuit, there being no large and equipped theatres and auditoria at all in the major cities. These all came later, as the provinces and Canada celebrated various anniversaries. However, Walter Homburger had done his best for us, and we now also had engaged David Haber as production stage manager.

As is customary when companies make their initial visit to a theatre (though I can barely bring myself to use that word in this context), David sent the managers a questionnaire on such matters as the dimensions of the stage, the number of lines for hanging scenery and lighting pipes, the number of dressing rooms, the seating capacity, the orchestra pit, and so on. Some theatres have a rail attached to balconies from which one can hang front-of-house lights; so we also asked 'Do you have a balcony rail?' One irate manager replied, 'Of course we have a balcony rail, and in all other respects the theatre is perfectly safe.'

However, such premonitions of difficulties were becoming easier to accept, and we were a happy group when we all set out for our first engagement at Calgary. As was usual, we travelled by train (and on this occasion we had a coach to ourselves), so that our effects would travel free. Three days and two nights on the train, and a performance the evening we arrived at Calgary! This worried me, as the dancers' legs would inevitably stiffen up from such a long period of inactivity, and I was most anxious that they dance well on their western debut. The dancers were aware of the importance of their mission, but most of them were very excited and regarded the trip as a great lark.

Being in the same car for three days and nights (we did have sleeping berths) generated that warm community or family

The village boys tease Dr Coppélius in the
two-act production in the second season

Scenes from the complete *Coppélia* presented for the first time in the 1958-59 season. Lilian Jarvis and Earl Kraul were still playing Swanilda and Franz respectively, and Howard Meadows was the Burgomaster. Howard is still with the company, in the wardrobe department, where his patience with Rudolf Nureyev was later much admired

atmosphere which is, I believe, unique to theatrical companies and which is a rare joy to experience. We had our little jokes and adventures. Once when our company manager, Richard Butterfield, a fastidious dresser, took off for the washroom in his silk pyjamas and dressing gown, we (yes, I admit I was party to it) stole his fedora from his berth and all tried it on; somehow, it never looked the same again. (Dick, if you read this, please forgive me.)

Kay Ambrose was with us on this trip, working (and being paid) as our public relations officer, though still designing free sets and costumes for us. She and I taught some of the company the lyrics, sung to Dvorak's 'Humoresque,' which had resounded through the crowded troop-trains of wartime Britain:

Passengers will please refrain
From passing water while the train is standing
In the station. I love you.

Men who're working underneath
Will catch it in the eyes and teeth,
So hold it in – or do it in your shoe.

One of the stations where we stopped was at Moose Jaw. It was dark, but a number of dancers left the train in search of coffee and to stretch their legs. When they returned, they looked guilty, and I wondered if they'd had a few beers; but I decided that they could not have afforded them. After a while, they sheepishly placed a gorgeous fluffy Persian cat in my lap, assuring me that it was a stray they had rescued from the platform. They named it Salome, after the ballet in our repertoire, and we spent the rest of the tour hiding her from train conductors. What a life that poor cat had – looked after by dancers in turns, locked in hotel rooms, carried around under people's coats, with different 'homes' and 'parents' every few days. But she survived the trip and

Lois and David in the pas de deux
from the third act of *Coppélia*

only broke down several months later in Toronto – a true westerner! – and we had unfortunately to put our unofficial mascot out of her misery.

The train reached Calgary about 7.30 on the morning of 27 October, and we were to perform that evening in the Grand theatre. We all rushed there for a loosening-up class and a rehearsal of that night's program – the first and second acts of *Coppélia* and our old reliable, the *Polovtsian Dances*. It was not a full house, but the audience was enthusiastic. For the following afternoon we had planned a 2.30 matinée for school children, but they did not get out of school till 3.30 – a fact that our sponsors, the Calgary Symphony Orchestra, had overlooked – and we had only a small house. There was much both we and our local sponsors had to learn, usually the hard way.

Take printed programs for example. In one town, I was horrified to find that no house programs had been printed: there we were, trying to bring ballet to a virgin and sceptical audience but looking so unprofessional and insulting the public by keeping them ignorant of the program and the names of the dancers. We had almost no petty cash, the promoter would not pay, so Dick Butterfield had to arrange for mimeographed sheets to be handed out.

At Edmonton, I had my first confrontation with the Musicians' Union. Nowadays the union and the company understand one another, for no Canadian theatrical organization has created and continues to create more employment for musicians than the National Ballet, and I respect the union's stand in protecting the rights of their members. But back in 1952 I found myself being forced to allow eight musicians to play for our Edmonton performances. Since we were carrying our two-piano team (George Crum and June McBride), we had, of course, no orchestral parts with us. I found it difficult to understand how these musicians had conceived they could sightread eight different ballets (including the world premiere of *Le Pommier* and the notoriously difficult *L'Après-midi d'un faune*). It shocked me that they showed no understanding of our financial or artistic concerns and that artistic standard was considered of no importance whatsoever.

However, I talked them out of playing the ballets; they then wanted to play 'light' music in the pit while the audience assembled. I was not going to have that either: how could an audience get in the mood for Chopin or Tchaikovsky by listening to 'Tea for Two'? But the musicians had a contract with the school auditorium in which we were to perform; I thought that if I paid them then, at least, they would go away! But no – they insisted on playing. Eventually we found a compromise whereby they played in the foyer and, thank God, I could not hear them. They had had their names – all eight of

them! – printed in *our* program under the title of the 'Edmonton Orchestra.' The nerve!

But there were good things about our first visit to Edmonton. Mrs Hazel Cristall was chairman of the National Ballet Committee in the city, and when we stumbled off the train at 6.30 in the morning, she had organized a more than decent breakfast and booked us into a passable hotel; she had seen that advertising had been sold in the house program; and after our performance that evening (30 October) she held a reception at her house at which – joy of joys – there was hot food.

Our appreciation of these arrangements was greatly heightened by our experiences between our visit to Calgary and our début in Edmonton. After the last performance in Calgary on 28 October, we climbed aboard a train at 11.45 pm, and arrived at Red Deer at 2.35 am, when our car was shunted off to a siding and began to cool down considerably.

To keep warm, we soon had to drag our freezing feet off to the station; but one of the girls was ill, and she had to be left in the cold car; another girl tried to take food for her and had to walk miles, looking for the car which had been shunted off elsewhere.

We were giving matinée and evening performances at the recently constructed Red Deer Memorial Centre, under the sponsorship of the Red Deer Quota Club. The lady representing the sponsor became very angry when she found we were not erecting any scenery. She told David Haber that she had only engaged us because we had scenery – and where was it? David told her that we had indeed laboriously brought our scenery from the depot as usual and that it was on the truck outside the stage door. The door, however, was the same size as the normal door in a house, not big enough for the scenery to be carried through. David opened the door, and they looked out: there was the truck, as

promised. So was a cow.

Our breakfast had been an unappetizing one in a 'greasy spoon,' and by the time the matinée was over, the company was ravenous for the meal promised us before the evening show. A fleet of cars had been arranged to take us to a sort of drill hall, heated by a wood stove; the car in which I and some colleagues were seated proceeded at a surprisingly slow pace and seemed strangely 'posh' given the other amenities of the town. It gradually dawned on us that it must be a hearse, which could never be seen, of course, travelling through the streets at a normal speed.

We eventually arrived at the hall to find some very thick white-bread sandwiches filled with something or other. On that, we danced our way through the evening performance; we looked for a restaurant, but none was open; so we clambered exhausted into our refrigerated coach and were hauled away to Edmonton

Giselle's costume was designed by Kay Ambrose from prints of the original French production

Scenes from the second production of *Giselle,* first seen in our 1956-57 season. The two top photographs on this page are of Adams and Franca as Loys/Albrecht and Giselle; Lois Smith is Queen of the Wilis on the far left and below, showing photo-calls of Act II. The 'universal' was behind the scrim in the photograph below

about three in the morning.

Red Deer was probably our toughest engagement, but we kept up a gruelling pace. An evening performance in Vancouver, an overnight trip on the ferry to Victoria, rehearsal in the afternoon, performance in the evening; so it went on. Nowadays, this kind of schedule would just not be allowed by the unions. But, despite the terrible conditions, our morale remained high and I don't recall any serious grumbling.

Our last performance was at Fort William on 24 November. All in all, we gave twenty-five performances in four weeks in eleven different towns or cities – which, given the conditions, now seems to me a practically incomprehensible achievement.

# New Ballets

The extent of the repertoire we took on that western tour also strikes me now as remarkable. The classics were represented by the first and second acts of *Coppélia*, *Les Sylphides*, the *Dances* from 'Prince Igor,' the second act of *The Nutcracker*, and both acts of *Giselle*. The newer ballets were *L'Après-midi d'un faune*, *Etude* by Kay Armstrong, *Ballet behind Us* by David Adams, and *Le Pommier* (on which more below). Thus, even in Vancouver where we gave four performances, we did not have to repeat any program completely.

Once back in Toronto, we added two further works – *Ballet Composite*, already mentioned (which was arranged for our two pianists since our own orchestra was too small to tackle the full Brahms orchestration), and Antony Tudor's masterpiece, *Jardin aux lilas.*

Of all our ballets at that time, *Lilas* was best suited to the company. We had an excellent cast. Lois Smith as Caroline came nearer in quality to the original – the sensi-tive and delicate Maude Lloyd – than any other dancer I have seen; and David Adams as her Lover was strong and blessed with good timing. James Ronaldson, who had by now joined the company, gave dignity to the role of the Man She Must Marry. And I danced the Woman in His Past – a part that contained some tricky lifts in our pas de deux; but Jimmy was as superb a partner then as he is a wardrobe supervisor now.

This was a role which, when I was with the Ballet Rambert, I had the good fortune to inherit from Peggy van Praagh and to learn from Antony Tudor himself and from Hugh Laing who first danced the Lover. Their instructions were incredibly clear. Steps were taught with explicit emphasis on the style of movement, which was in turn dictated by the Edwardian setting and the Woman's character; certain movements would thus have to be made on specific beats, while others would flow in long phrases through the music, yet ending on a

A later cast for *Jardin aux lilas:* Jocelyn Terelle as Caroline, Earl Kraul as Her Lover, Yves Cousineau as the Man She Must Marry, and Jacqueline Ivings as the Woman in His Past

The first production of *Jardin aux lilas* (1953-54), with Lois Smith, David Adams, and Celia Franca

definite beat. A turn of the head would have to be just so: too much or too little would distort the meaning of the character. They also demanded that a dancer be continually aware of his or her position on stage – how far to the left or right, how deep into the stage to travel, where to be in relation to the other dancers, and *why*. Although I don't think I had more than two or three rehearsals with them, what they taught me was invaluable, especially when it became my duty in later years to teach others.

I then learned all the roles in *Jardin aux lilas*, simply because the ballet fascinated me. But when I came to teach it to the Canadian company some fifteen years later, a few pieces of the choreography had escaped me; fortunately Tudor was at that time rehearsing the New York City Ballet in a revival of the work, and I was able to join him to refresh my memory of this romantic work.

In creating my first Canadian ballet, however, I was not so successful. When I came to Canada, I was advised very strongly that the company had to gain the support of French Canada; so, in all innocence, not having digested very much Canadian history, I proceeded quickly to fabricate a naive but well-intentioned pastiche. This was *Le Pommier*. Both Kay Ambrose and George Crum were bilingual, and they helped me greatly in researching the background. Kay designed the décor and the costumes, after taking a great fancy to handwoven rugs from Quebec; a well-known tenor from Quebec City, Pierre Boutet, helped to select some French-Canadian folk songs; and George invited composer Hector Gratton to write a score based on them. From the lyrics I made up a gentle scenario incorporating the activities of a fiddler, a milkmaid, an old man, a cobbler, a baker and his wife and children, a miller and his wife and daughters, and two labourers. The action took place in a village presumed to have been inhabited by forefathers of contemporary French-Canadians.

There were two Montrealers dancing in the ballet, Brian Mac-Donald and André Dufresne. A member of the board of the guild and a professor at the Université de Montréal, André Bachand, attended the première, which, as I have said, occurred at Edmonton, and he seemed pleased. So were the Edmonton critics: *Le Pommier* was 'unpretentious,' yet 'entertaining' and 'well received.' And on other performances during our western tour, it was accepted for what it was – light entertainment and a sincere, friendly gesture to French-speaking Canadians.

Why not, therefore, take it to Montreal on our next visit there? This we did, performing it in February 1953 at Her Majesty's theatre. The audiences seemed to enjoy it for what it was, accepting that it was 'as little Canadian as the Scottish dance in *Coppélia* was Scottish.' The critics, French and English, were courteous about the work's merits; one called it 'un joli divertissement,' for example; they devoted a great deal of space to the work, however, lending it an importance it did not warrant.

But there were some members of the Montreal branch, very sensitive to cultural matters, who surprised me by feeling incensed and insulted that I should portray such a simple *habitant* image of Quebec. So, like *Salome*, *Le Pommier* was soon withdrawn from the repertoire.

I was learning...

In January 1953 we made a brave move. The guild shifted the company to the Royal Alexandra theatre (known to all affectionately as 'the Royal Alex' or even 'the Alex'), then Toronto's sole show-case for stage shows of any pretension. It had been built in an Edwardian style for dramas with fairly small casts, so it suffered from the disadvantage that there were few dressing rooms on stage level; consequently most of the dancers had to run up and down several flights of stone stairs – and this several times a day, since we held our rehearsals and classes there too. Their legs suffered as a result.

One other difficulty, apart from its costing more to rent than the Eaton auditorium, was that, having been a drama house, it had no orchestra pit. The musicians' instruments would stick up above the level of the stage, spoiling the view of those in the front rows. Perhaps the only person not to complain was Muriel Crum, George's mother, whose eyes were not very good anyway; she used to like to sit behind her son in the front row and, smiling beatifically, just listen to the music.

Though the stage of 'the Alex' wasn't very large, yet it was well proportioned, and the theatre, for an aging legitimate house, was fairly well equipped. It was to be our home for the next ten years, and they were very prolific ones. Kay Ambrose designed and I staged ballets without any payment, and our choreographers also created for nothing. Our production costs were kept to the minimum, and the company just managed to continue to scrape by financially.

I remember one occasion when Betty Oliphant, who became our ballet mistress in that second season, and myself, armed with a couple of bottles, invited Ernest Rawley, the Alex manager, and Edwin De Rocher, the box-office manager, into my dressing room after a performance. Our intentions were not honourable. We were both proud that, in spite of our touch-and-go finances, we had always paid the dancers on time; but a Friday was coming up and there was no money, since the rental of theatre had first claim on the box-office receipts. By the end of the two bottles, we had all agreed that the dancers had first priority and the two weeks' rental could wait.

A photo-call shot of the final scene of
*Jardin aux lilas* with the first cast in their
exact choreographed positions. James
Ronaldson, as the Man She Must Marry, is
leading off Lois Smith, leaving David
Adams right centre and Celia Franca far
left

Ernie and Ed were tough managers, but they really believed in us. Ernie was one of the few theatre managers left at that time who still loved theatre. Many times after a performance Betty Oliphant and I would sit in his front-of-house office and listen to him tell stories of the famous artists he had welcomed to the Alex – people like Alexandra Danilova and Frederic Franklin from the Ballets Russes de Monte Carlo, and Margot Fonteyn with the Sadler's Wells Ballet.

The company now would perform in a theatre with the right tradition to it.

*An Eastern Tour*

We opened at the Royal Alex in January 1953 and played for a whole week, dancing all the works in our repertoire. And then we were off touring again, first to southern Ontario, then to Montreal (when *Le Pommier* was hit by the frost), and on to eastern Canada – Fredericton, Saint John, Sydney, Halifax, Sackville, and Quebec City. We gave our first performance in Ottawa on the way back and visited three other Ontario towns before settling down in Toronto again.

What I remember most vividly of this tour are again our introductions to auditoriums never intended for a performance by a ballet company. Any group which has not played in the Devon School auditorium in Fredericton has not lived. The stage seemed miles wide and inches deep, so the audience there saw a production of *Les Sylphides* which must be unique in its history. The traditional vertical lines of sylphs on either side of the stage had to be arranged as diago-nals, and as I changed straight lines and semi-circles to flat inverted Vs I prayed that Fokine would look down upon me mercifully.

In the sixties, if I may leap forward in time, Fredericton also received a new theatre, built by Lord Beaverbrook, so it is said, to please his wife. We performed in it for the first time in 1967, but it proved little better than the Devon School auditorium. Lady Beaver-brook had not liked the exterior design: there was a large square box rising above the roofline to which she objected. So that bit was left out in the construction. Unfor-tunately, it was intended to house the flies, where the scenery and lighting pipes are 'flown' in and out. When the Beaverbrooks were both dead, it was discovered that the flies could legally be added and other improvements made. The flies were duly built – and painted on the outside in bright psyche-delic colours which can be seen for miles around rising above the trees.

Yves Cousineau, Celia Franca, and Ray Moller in Elizabeth Leese's *The Lady from the Sea*

*Barbara Allen.* The top photograph shows David Adams in his own 1960-61 version, and the others show the production danced in the 1950s. David was the Witch Boy in both versions; Jury Gotshalks is the leaping fundamentalist preacher far left

When these renovations had been completed, a celebratory musical show was in order, and so an orchestra was required. An advance representative of this visiting show arrived, and asked where the pit was.

'Under the stage.'

'Where does the conductor go?'

'Oh, he goes down under too.'

It appears to have been thought that the conductor did not have to be able to see the stage or cue in performers or accompany them! This structural oversight was remedied by taking a jack hammer and knocking out a two-foot square hole in a thick cement block near the front of the stage. So, if a conductor rose through the hole like a jack-in-the-box to conduct the performers on stage, he thereby could not – unless with his navel – conduct the underground orchestra at the same time.

These extraordinary facilities were not used by our company until October 1974, when we arrived with our own orchestra.

George Crum, whose girth was then rather larger than the hole had been designed for, stayed underground most of the time, so that the orchestra could see his arm movements. For stage cues, he would stand on tiptoe and, then visible from the nose up, cue the dancers with his eyes. For really important cues, like the beginnings and ends of solos, he'd try one hand above stage and the other in the dungeon. There was another complication: the grand piano, which would not get into the basement, was on George's left in a sort of ante-room, so situated that our pianist, Mary McDonald, and George could not see each other; Mary prayed that she would get entries and tempi right, and George occasionally produced a convulsive movement to the left, in the hope that Mary could see his beat.

The only entrance to the concrete dungeon for the orchestra in the Beaverbrook theatre is through a trapdoor cut in the floor upstage

Antony Tudor's *Gala Performance,* to music by Prokofiev, finely satirized the conduct of prima ballerinas—Russian, Italian, and French—around the turn of the century. Lois Smith as the Italian ballerina, followed by her dresser; below, the finale

right and down a spiral staircase. Norman Dyson, then our production stage manager, held the door up while the musicians descended one at a time. As the last man went down he lowered it, with the cry to the deck below, 'All right, now row, you bastards!'

Somehow, the company managed to keep fairly well in time...

One other lasting impression I have of that 1953 tour to the Maritimes is our visit to Sackville. We arrived from Halifax and, since we were going on to Quebec City by overnight train, had no other base but the theatre on the campus of Mount Allison University. It was a big, draughty hall with a dark brown feel to it. It had a flat floor, so that, unless you were seated in the front row, it was difficult to see the stage. Like every other place we played in, the hall was practically unheated; the chill was dangerous, for dancers' muscles must be kept warm to help avoid injuries. I therefore developed a technique of arguing, politely at first, with any local manager or janitor I could find and, if I failed at that, of 'throwing a temperament' and threatening to withdraw the company. This often worked, because there would be a powerful local organization – the Kiwanis or Rotary Club – sponsoring the performance.

Once we had the heat turned on at Sackville, the next problem was the organ, a massive array of pipes ranging across the entire back of the 'stage.' It made a hideous background but there were no flies from which to hang our backdrop. Above the roof was the great outdoors. Kay Ambrose and David Haber got in touch with some students from the university's art department who were to act as stage hands; we fixed our old blue skycloth to a metal pipe and tied lengths of rope to each end; the boys gallantly went out in the cold, climbed on to the roof, and bored holes in it through which the ropes could be passed and knotted. Thus

Robert Ito

A photo-call shot of *Offenbach in the Underworld* just before the cancan

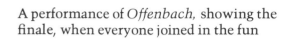

A performance of *Offenbach,* showing the finale, when everyone joined in the fun

Studio photographs for *Offenbach*. Antony Tudor chose the cancan dancers for the length of their legs and specified that exactly five inches of flesh should show above their black stockings. Jacqueline Ivings (centre), usually so modest and demure, surprised everyone by her spirited dancing of the cancan

the organpipes were concealed.

Under the stage was the one and only dressing room, an ill-lit and freezing area with a floor (and sanitary arrangements!) of simple brown earth. The students obligingly went off to fetch us some hot coffee, they found pieces of cardboard to put under the dancers' feet while they made up and so prevent their ballet shoes from becoming soiled, they hung up a sheet to divide the place into boys' and girls' dressing areas, and they put up strings of naked light bulbs. Electric heaters were found, as were bowls of water so that the dancers could remove their makeup after the performance. I don't think I was very popular for insisting that the dancers wear their body make-up as usual in these circumstances.

But out of the miserable discomfort of the whole operation there was born a splendid rapport between dancers and students. The audience responded well, never having seen anything like us in that dull, depressing hall. When all was over, dancers and students alike shared a glowing sense of accomplishment and went contentedly off into the night together in search of a restaurant. I still have a very soft spot for Mount Allison.

# Touring in the United States

By 1953, the news of the company's existence had spread to the United States; we received an invitation from Ted Shawn, director of the famous Jacob's Pillow Dance Festival in Massachusetts, to perform there during the first week of August that year.

The thing that stands out in my mind about this, our first US engagement, is how pretty the girls looked. I was proud that their legs were so long and slim, for I had seen too many lumpy, muscle-bound examples resulting from bad training. The men were clean-cut without being boring.

There was also my run-in with Anatole Chujoy, the editor-owner of New York's *Dance News*. He wanted our company to participate in the Regional Dance Festivals; I did not. He never forgave me, and I felt his ire for years to come.

And I recall the rehearsals of *Lilac Garden* (*Jardin aux lilas*) with Antony Tudor (who was a resident summer-time teacher there along with the well-known British teacher Margaret Craske, an exponent of Maestro Enrico Cecchetti's system of training). Tudor was very interested in Lois and David, who were to dance Caroline and her Lover, and seemed very much to enjoy rehearsing them. He also, I suspect, was secretly pleased to have his work performed with the dedication and respect we gave it. I think he adored adoration.

Tudor's style of instruction is well known to those who have worked with him. Some masochistic artists love him for it; others of us put up with it because his finished ballets are powerful works of art and because he challenges our intellect by his demands and activates our imaginations by his descriptions of character. He made Judie Colpman rehearse an entrance time and time again, making cutting remarks after every try. She was near to tears, but she didn't actually cry.

He also wanted me to do a difficult lift with Jimmy Ronaldson,

Lawrence Adams and Lois Smith in
*Swan Lake*

Franca's four-act version of *Swan Lake* premiered in the company's fourth season. Left, Act III, the ballroom scene, with the 'universal' in use in the bottom photograph. Below, Lois Smith as Odile and David Kerval as von Rothbart

Photo-calls of the second act showing the original backdrop. It was later damaged by rain while in storage and a backdrop from *Les Sylphides* had to be used instead

Lois Smith and David Adams, as the lovers temporarily reunited in the fourth act of *Swan Lake*

taking off for the jump from the left foot. I was then thirty-two years of age and had been taking off from the right leg every time I danced the role since my early teens when I first learned it from Tudor himself. My mind said 'Take off from the left foot,' but my muscles refused to comply. Antony insisted I get it right then and there. Jimmy Ronaldson's left arm had just about turned to jelly by the time my body eventually obeyed.

Ted Shawn's budget for his performances was not big, so an orchestra was out of the question (as it was, we had taken only about half the dancers with us). Rather than perform *Lilas* to a recording, we brought violinist Morry Kernerman to play Ernest Chausson's 'Poème,' and George Crum and June McBride were our two-piano team for all our other productions – *Coppélia* Act II, *The Nutcracker* Act II, *Faune,* the peasant pas de deux from *Giselle,* and the *Don Quixote* pas de deux.

All told, we were a success. The dancers' unpretentiousness was refreshing to an audience which was used to fireworks and circus tricks in classical pas de deux and had a preference for modern dance. Of course, Tudor was (and is) a genius, and his *Lilac Garden* and our interpretation of it were acclaimed.

So began our frequent US tours. In 1955 we became the first Canadian cultural activity to be booked for American tours by a leading agency. Walter Homburger arranged to have us signed up with the William Morris Agency of New York. We came under the Special Attractions division, which was run by Klaus Kolmar. Klaus was a friend for many years. He believed in our company and did his best to sell us to nation-wide managers. We had a potentially marketable repertoire by then, but we could not command a big fee because we were unknowns from Canada, which, as a country itself, was also as good as unknown.

I secretly suffered on these tours from an ever-present consciousness of our shortcomings. At first we could afford only two pianos for accompaniment, and later a pitifully small touring orchestra sawing, blowing, and banging away at Tchaikovsky, Delibes, Chausson, Prokofiev, Debussy, Adam, Appelbaum, Borodin, and Chopin. The lighting equipment we carried was minimal, and sadly most theatres had little usable equipment of their own. Nevertheless, we gradually built up an excellent reputation with the impresarios and concert managers, most of whom requested return engagements every two years.

Touring conditions were excruciatingly uncomfortable at times. We always did things the cheapest way: we hired the cheapest buses with the worst-paid drivers, and we hired the cheapest company managers (we had to hire one under the regulations of the Association of Theatrical Press Agents and Managers); some were drunk or crazy or aged or even all three. We seldom had the money to send our stage crew on in advance of the company in order to make such arrangements as unloading the trucks which carried our effects, handling scenery and lights, allotting dressing rooms to artists, ensuring that the heat was turned on backstage, and setting up our portable practice *barres* for the dancers' warm-up exercises.

The William Morris Agency sometimes booked dates for us on college circuits or in community concert series, and on these we would receive a guaranteed fee. In order to fill out a tour, the agency needed to add a number of engagements where we would share in the receipts on a percentage basis. Our board understandably procrastinated for months, deciding whether or not to gamble on those dates. Meanwhile we could not offer contracts to musicians and stage hands, or book trucks and buses and drivers, or let the dancers know what kind of

Below, the first full-length *Nutcracker:* a photo-call shot with Marcel Chojnacki as Drosselmeyer; left, the Russian Dance

Stage shots of *The Nutcracker* at the Royal Alex during the latter half of the fifties: top left are the Oriental Dance, and the Sugar Plum Fairy and the Prince; below left is Clara during the battle between the Gingerbreads and the Mice, and right shows the Kingdom of Sweets

The Snow Queen waving goodbye
to Clara sitting in a sleigh pulled by
reindeer

The nocturne from *Les Sylphides*

*Dark Elegies* is a Tudor ballet to Mahler's haunting song-cycle, 'Kindertotenlieder.' Above is Celia Franca in the first song, and below are Lois Smith held aloft and David Adams kneeling in the second. This was the first of the NBC ballets in which projection was used, to float the clouds on the backdrop. The costumes were modelled on those designed for its London premiere by Nadia Benois, mother of Peter Ustinov

Glenn Gibson, Angela Leigh, and Ray Moller pose in a scene from David Adams' most successful ballet, *Pas de chance.* Below, the company's first ballet by Frederick Ashton, *Les Rendez-vous*

season to expect. Klaus Kolmar kept concert managers dangling as long as possible, but by the time the board of directors had decided, he had had to switch the dates around several times. So instead of geographically ordered engagements we often zigzagged erratically, adding hundreds of extra miles to our travels in the States.

We were nervous and apprehensive even prior to setting out on our annual American wanderings. We had no full-time rehearsal studio or workshops in Toronto. Late in every October we were obliged to vacate the St Lawrence Hall to make way for the homeless and unemployed. Directors and staff alike would walk the streets in the rain searching for empty buildings which looked as if they might have suitable space rentable for a song. We would find ourselves some mornings rehearsing on the waxed floor of a nightclub, breathing in the left-over fumes from the night before; or we would be in a remote parish hall in north Toronto. For a time, we were very well looked after by a ballet teacher, Bettina Byers, and her assistant, Marjorie Haskins, who allowed us to use their studio rent-free until their own students arrived around four in the afternoon.

Jack Brockie obtained a room for a while in Margaret Eaton School, where our costumes could be made. Otherwise, makeshift arrangements were made wherever the dancers rehearsed, or in our homes or the seamstresses' homes. When we eventually acquired our own administrative office, all our activities seemed to occur miles away from it, and communication was always a problem.

One miserable place we rented for a long time was in the eastern side of the city, on Pape Avenue. It consisted of two ramshackle rooms joined by a corridor, and it was situated over a feed and grain store. One room was used for rehearsals; its floor boards had great gaps between them through

*Winter Night,* with Donald Mahler and Jocelyn Terelle as the young lovers and Celia Franca as the discarded and unhappy Felice

122

Lois Smith also played Felice (top right);
below is a photo-call shot

Scenes from *The Mermaid* by Andrée Howard, originally created for the Ballet Rambert to a selection of Ravel's music. Above is the underwater scene where the Mermaid, Angela Leigh, acquires human legs, and below she steps out of the sea with hopes of princely love—which are, of course, not fulfilled

David Adams in the Nijinsky role of
Harlequin and Lois Smith as Columbine in
*Le Carnaval*

*Le Carnaval,* with original choreography for Diaghilev by Fokine. Stanislas Idzikowski, who taught the ballet to Celia Franca, had shared the leading male role with Nijinsky; Kay Ambrose reproduced the décor and costumes by Leon Bakst

A *Carnaval* photo-call

Grant Strate's *The Fisherman and His Soul*
danced to music by Harry Somers. Earl
Kraul is the Fisherman, Harold da Silva his
Soul, Angela Leigh (borne aloft) is the
Witch, and Lilian Jarvis the Mermaid

A studio shot of Sylvia Mason and Robert Ito in Brian Macdonald's *Post Script.* Below is the cast of *La Llamada* with Betty Pope on high and Ray Moller, the choreographer

Opposite, Jacqueline Ivings and Earl Kraul in Balanchine's *Concerto Barocco,* and the finale of *Pineapple Poll,* in which Auntie Dimple, dolled up to represent Britannia, is rotated by four jolly seamen

which a strong aroma rose from below. The store was unheated, so we also received blasts of cold air through the floor and were never able to get our feet warmed up. The second room was used by me and the stage manager as an office and also for building properties and storing wardrobe boxes. There was also a garret, where we put the costume department. The seamstresses and cutters over-looked this gloomy second room, disbelieving everything – the smell, the cold, the activities, and their own discomfort.

We didn't experience the luxury of a pre-tour dress rehearsal for many years; such was our penury that the dancers never rehearsed with the orchestra or on a stage with full scenery and lights. We would arrange for the dancers to attend the orchestra's 'note' rehearsals, and George was as accommodating as possible in trying to assess how much time he would rehearse each score so that dancers would not need to hang around if they were not cast in a certain ballet. We also managed to bring new costumes over to the current rehearsal studio so that the dancers could actually practise while wearing them.

The first few performances on the road were thus always nerve-racking. After hours of travel, our knees were so stiff we could hardly stagger off the bus. Many times our journeys took twice as long as necessary owing to the incompe-tence of the company manager or bus driver whose duty it was to navigate. Since the theatre season in North America is from late autumn to early spring, we often encountered blizzards and more than once ended up in a ditch. It was difficult to rise above the sheer physical discomfort of it all and transform ourselves into creatures of beauty in time for 'curtain up.'

Even when our tours took us down south to Florida or Cali-fornia, where the sun shone, we were not rid of our problems. Some dancers could not resist the

The National Ballet holds up Washington in various ways. The parade at the bottom is passing the house of Robert Farquharson in Georgetown; he gave us the greatest and friendliest possible support on our first visit

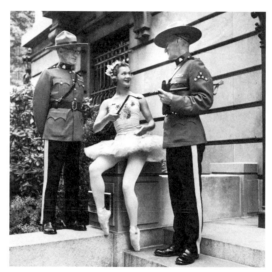

Opposite, a specially posed grouping of the dancers in *L'Après-midi d'un faune,* taken in the Rock Creek Park in Washington, DC

swimming and sunbathing and would arrive at the theatre debilitated from the unaccustomed heat and with sunburns which shone through the heaviest applications of wet white.

It was essential that we arranged publicity photos to send home to Canada showing the dancers having 'fun in the sun' while acting as Canadian cultural ambassadors. Our appearances during the summer at the Carter Barron Amphitheatre in Washington, DC, were typical of this situation. We understood the importance of performing in the US capital and brought Ken Bell along to take photographs. It was hell rehearsing on the open stage during the heat and humidity of the day, but even worse were the photo calls which Ken and Kay set up. There was no relief from the humidity and the incredibly high temperatures, but the company spirit was such that the dancers, without complaint, did what they knew they had to do for the 'good of the cause.' And we

did get some fine photographs, which served the company well for immediate newspaper coverage at home and as future material for souvenir programs and general publicity.

These perfomances in the United States were vital for the National Ballet for various reasons: Canada's population was too small then to support a long season of employment, for one thing, and this inhibited the development of a permanent company or of a real company at all. The costs of transportation for Canadian coast-to-coast tours were too high when measured against the income they generated; so we had to try for the US audiences who had been attending ballet performances for years. In Canada we were still trying to create an audience, and the fact of US recognition, given the Canadian inferiority complex, then helped us to succeed at home. When we first arrived in Washington, the Canadian embassy trembled. The ambassador,

Arnold Heeney, had purchased a block of seats for our opening performance and invited representatives from many embassies to attend. The Canadians had never seen us dance and were understandably apprehensive. Would we disgrace them? Well, of course, we did not, and Heeney's sigh of relief was almost audible.

*On Television*

Opposite, Jocelyn Terelle in
*Concerto Barocco*

During the late 1940s in London it had been my good fortune to work with two men of vision: Cecil McGivern, a head of television programming for the British Broadcasting Corporation, and Christian Simpson, a producer-director. McGivern had courageously commissioned a ballet tailored to the potential of the new medium of television. Whether it was design or chance I don't know, but putting me and Chris Simpson together as collaborators turned out to be good 'casting.' Chris' lively imagination and downright love for the medium positively inspired me.

By today's standards of technology, our two productions, *The Dance of Salome* and *The Eve of St Agnes,* would doubtless appear naive, but in those days at Alexandra Palace, affectionately known as 'Ally Pally,' when television was still in its infancy, they were historical landmarks.

My initial interest in television was sparked by curiosity. From a purely artistic viewpoint I was intrigued by the possibility of producing dance within new disciplines. In years to come, my concerns with Canadian television were – in addition to the artistic ones – with securing extra employment for our dancers and with reaching a larger audience than the ballet could command in theatres.

However, when I arrived in Canada in 1951 clutching a letter of introduction from Cecil McGivern to Fergus Mutrie, his counterpart in Toronto, television was not yet in operation. We had to wait until 1954, when the Canadian Broadcasting Corporation presented us in Antony Tudor's *Gala Performance* with the pas de trois from *Swan Lake* as a time filler. Our producer was the very musical Franz Kraemer. Studio Four in Toronto, where we did the first show, was miserably small, and, while we may have deserved A for effort, the result was not a great artistic success. The second program he produced a few years later

included Tudor's *Lilac Garden*
and *Offenbach in the Underworld*;
it was no better.

In December 1956, however, I
met my second Chris Simpson,
the brilliant producer-director
Norman Campbell. We collaborated on fourteen shows between
1956 and 1975. During all those
years I cannot recall one cross word
ever passing between us – which
must be some kind of a record
considering the tensions inherent
in the television business. Dancers, cameramen, sound technicians, musicians – all respected
Norman for his imaginative and
daring ideas about new techniques
and for his consideration towards
all who worked with him. He was
so secure in his talent that I could
uninhibitedly put forward my own
suggestions without fear of being
misunderstood.

Many producers, it has to be said,
work defensively, mistaking such
suggestions for criticisms. They
flounder around at rehearsals,
wasting union time and dancers'
energies while deciding which
camera should take a pas de chat
and from which angle. It is frustrating sitting in a control booth
watching the dancers on the TV
monitors being photographed from
bad angles so that their legs appear
fat and foreshortened or a close-up
exaggerates the worst features of a
face. The inexperienced or insensitive director may not even notice a
dancer's wrists disappearing above
the screen or the ankles cut off
below it, or he may even decide it
doesn't matter, just at the moment
when the hands and feet are
expressing an emotion vital to the
action.

I lived in dread of what I call
'crotch shots' when, for example,
the male dancer lifts the ballerina
high in the air with her legs in a
split. The lift may be carried from
audience (or camera) right to left,
the choreography obviously having
been designed to be seen from
centre front. The producer, because
the action travels left, is liable to

have the camera in the left corner of the studio take the shot (and from a low angle!), so that what is seen by the viewer is a crotch advancing towards him at a rate of knots and filling more and more of the screen. If one dares to complain, one might well be told, 'But that's the way it is.' Perhaps, but it is not the choreographic intention and it is certainly not art – just tastelessness and ignorance.

More often than not, dance professionals enter into a TV production with a lazy, selfish attitude: 'I'm here and will dance (or here is my ballet); now it's up to you to make me (or my ballet) look divine; but of course I won't change anything from the stage version.' There is trouble caused by any such arrogance.

The ideal arrangement is that the choreographer (or choreographer's representative) and the director both appreciate the capabilities and limitations of both art forms. Subtle compromises can be made: perhaps a group pattern can be narrowed so that it remains within the span of a camera's lens; or a camera can be specially positioned to photograph a section of choreography to enhance its integral excitement.

I believe that the choreographer or choreographer's representative should think: 'If, while protecting a choreographer's intention, I can adapt the choreography so that television techniques are utilized to their maximum effect, we will produce an entertaining and artistic show which will bring credit to both the ballet and the television industries.' And the dancer should ideally approach television thinking, 'If I trust the director and (say) change the directions of my steps to face an "audience" which is not necessarily seated in the front of the studio as it would be in a theatre, but rather is seated all around and above me, I will be shown to advantage.' The only drawback to these approaches is that you may not find a Norman Campbell to be your director.

How often have I explained to other producer-directors that dancers can fall on a slippery surface! It's so obvious that such producers say 'yes, of course,' but then they do nothing at all about it and consider me temperamental and far too fussy. It still makes me angry when I think of the hours and weeks of tension and nerves and wasted creative energies spent dealing with these idiocies. It was no joy at all keeping dancers calm and composed while trying at the same time to persuade the insensitive that a slippery floor was recklessly dangerous.

On one occasion, soon after Martine van Hamel had won the gold medal in the junior section of the Bulgarian International Ballet Competition in July 1966, she and her partner, Hazaros Surmeyan, were to tape the *Corsair* pas de deux which Martine had danced in the competition. After a few tries, it was obvious they were finding it impossible even to stand upright on the studio floor provided. The tape was never used; we lost out on the positive publicity Canadian ballet should have received, and the CBC wasted its money on stage crew, musicians' rehearsals, and so on.

*Au contraire,* Norman Campbell and his chief designer, Robert Lawson, went to endless pains to try out several non-slip paints on the studio floor, and we did rather well as a result. Later, when colour was introduced on television, the extra heat of the lamps would draw what little oil there was out of the paint, and another slip problem had to be solved.

The lights would be turned off whenever possible during blocking and rehearsal sessions so the floor could cool off and dry up. It was also agreed that, even if the use of resin on the dancers' shoes marked the floor (which doesn't look good on TV) the dancers' well-being and confident performances took first priority. A little courtesy went a long way, and the dancers didn't then shower their resin around unnecessarily.

Karen Kain and television producer
Norman Campbell at a recent rehearsal
session in Studio 7

Long-time television colleagues and friends, Norman Campbell and Tom Farquharson on Camera Two. Below and opposite, the Capulets' ball from *Romeo and Juliet*; the décor for the television production was designed by Robert Lawson

Jeremy Blanton as the Carnival King in *Romeo and Juliet.* Below, the final group in the Citizens' dance; opposite, Mercutio (Lawrence Adams) dies after his duel with Tybalt (Yves Cousineau)

Celia Franca as Lady Capulet in the studio
and Veronica Tennant dancing Juliet

Lady Capulet, with thc Nurse (Angela
Leigh), happily receives flowers from
Juliet's bridesmaids on the morning of her
planned wedding to Paris; in the next
action the Nurse opens the curtains to
reveal Juliet lying apparently dead

Veronica Tennant and Earl Kraul as Romeo
in the death scene

Through Campbell's and Lawson's leadership and concern and because of the rapport built up between dancers, lighting and sound technicians, camera men, ballet masters, switchers, script assistants, make-up artists, and others, *everyone* did his or her best.

Between 1956 and 1959 we transmitted live five ballets under Norman Campbell's direction for the Canadian Broadcasting Corporation. The first was the complete *Swan Lake* (my version based on that I had learned from the Sadler's Wells Ballet) with Lois Smith and David Adams. In 1957 we performed the first two acts of *Coppélia* with Betty Pope as Swanilda, Earl Kraul as Franz, and Ray Moller as Dr Coppélius. Norman and I are cat-lovers, so we borrowed his Sylvester for Dr Coppélius to carry under his arm; Sylvester helped bring out both the sinister and endearing sides of Dr Coppélius' character. That season also saw a performance of *Winter Night,* the emotional ballet about a love

'triangle' with choreography by Walter Gore to Rachmaninov's second piano concerto.

Our first full-length *Nutcracker,* aired in December 1958, was a riot. We squeezed its hour and fifty minutes into one hour; though there were some cuts, George Crum had to conduct the music at an unbelievably fast tempo. The dancers were game but distinctly hard-pushed and smiling desperately. In December 1959 we televised our last live transmitted broadcast – John Cranko's *Pineapple Poll* with a visibly pregnant Lilian Jarvis as Poll, Lawrence Adams as Captain Belaye, and Patrick Hurde as Jasper the Pot Boy.

Later on when we taped *Cinderella* in 1968 (it then won an Emmy Award from the National Academy of Television and Sciences), Norman dreamed up some wonderful ideas using techniques new to the medium. Mary Jago, the Spring Fairy, flew out of a flower; Leeyan Granger, the Summer Fairy, emerged in slow motion from a

Lady Capulet has just given Juliet her first ballgown in the CBC prize-winning production

150

Top, a posed shot on the stage of the
O'Keefe centre from Erik Bruhn's version
of *Swan Lake,* with Elaine Crawford as the
Queen Mother. The other photographs are
of the television production: below, Erik
Bruhn with Lois Smith as the Black Swan;
below right, Veronica Tennant and Jeremy
Blanton in the Neapolitan dance created
specially for them by Bruhn; opposite
are Bruhn and Smith, with the lower
photograph showing them together with
the Swan Maidens towards the end of the
first lakeside scene

hot sun; Martine van Hamel, the Autumn Fairy, spun madly among swirling leaves. Many other such effects, all of which took time to plan, arrange, rehearse, and tape, were well worth the trouble and the dancers' patience in realizing the fairy-tale, fantasy-like quality of the story.

Union hours and TV studio time limited us, however, so that only a minimum amount of time could be spent explaining to the dancers in *Cinderella* the reasons *why,* for example, a certain jeté had to be executed from *this* piece of tape on the floor to *that* piece; I could only say, 'it will appear as though you are jumping from a cliff edge over an abyss to another cliff edge, darling.' Jeremy Blanton as the Prince and Lawrence Adams as his Aide were most helpful in thus creating for the TV camera the sequence in which the Prince and his companion journey around the world in search of Cinderella. Veronica Tennant as Cinderella was also most co-operative,

trusting us to do our best for her. We all ended up winners in competition with US productions – 'Sol Hurok Presents – Part III' (on the Columbia Broadcasting Service), 'Sounds of Summer' (Public Broadcasting Service), and 'Switched-on Symphony' (National Broadcasting Service).

One might have expected that our TV performances would become much easier once we were able to record on video-tape for future transmission; we could take breaks and we could replay the parts that did not succeed. But a new set of problems arose.

The rules of the several unions involved in producing a ballet had always been restricting, but now they had to be considered in relation to cost budgets prepared away in advance of production. We had to estimate how many hours of 'dry' rehearsal (that is, rehearsal in our own ballet rehearsal room without TV personnel and cameras) it would take to adapt the stage choreographies for television purposes. Each dancer was contracted separately for the number of hours he or she would work, and if we weren't careful a principal might earn less than a corps dancer who might be required for every scene and make several costume changes. A specific number of TV studio hours had to be booked for 'blocking' with cameras (that is, the dancers 'marking through' their moves without going full out, so that the camera men could accustom themselves to the dancers' positions and the dancers could orient themselves in the new décors and dimensions of the TV studio). Make-up and video-tape recording usually took place alternately with blocking sessions. If a section of the production wasn't going according to plan, there was then little time available for adjustment.

The schedules were so tight that, had I worked full-time for television, I would doubtless have ended up in a mental institution carrying around a giant watch and counting the seconds leading up to THE BIG SECOND – the moment after which thousands of dollars in overtime would have to be paid to dancers, musicians, stagehands, wardrobe assistants, sweeper-uppers, make-up artists, and all the others. It was very frustrating to find ourselves so confined and so burdened with large money considerations at the same time that we were creating and testing out these new techniques for television.

I have been speaking, of course, of television adaptations of productions originally created for the proscenium stage. It is to be hoped that funds will soon become available for Canadian productions to be specially commissioned for cameras. The ballet artists here must lead the way and lobby for this. The Europeans are already ahead in this area.

However, the CBC should be proud of having won the Prix René Barthelmy at the Monte Carlo International Competition in 1966

Right, Cinderella arrives at the ball during a stage performance; far right, her stepsisters sulk at the table, unaware of the presence of the Fairy Godmother; lower right, the stepsisters flirt at Prince Charming's ball

Below, the czardas from *Swan Lake*

for *Romeo and Juliet* in black and white with Earl Kraul and Veronica Tennant, and Emmy's for *Cinderella* in 1970 and Rudolf Nureyev's *Sleeping Beauty* in 1973. The CBC – whoever they are or it is – should know that we, the artists and technicians, were proud of our work and achievements – successes which then benefitted the CBC despite at times its lack of confidence and its apathy about providing adequate facilities.

We made our first video-tape of *Swan Lake* on 28 March 1961, with Smith and Adams (as in our previous live presentation) and with Yves Cousineau as von Rothbart, the evil magician. We wanted him to fly in and out of the scenes and so had him attached to a sort of Kirby's flying ballet apparatus; the fittings almost castrated him, but in the name of art he did not complain too much. We taped another version – Erik Bruhn's – in June 1967, which was presented during the holiday season at the end of that year. Bruhn and Smith led the cast, with a Black Queen replacing von Rothbart.

We did two versions of *Giselle,* both in colour – the first, taped in December 1961 and broadcast in December 1962, with Lois Smith as Giselle and Earl Kraul as Albrecht, Angela Leigh as the Queen of the Wilis, Yves Cousineau as Hilarion, and Sally Brayley riding a real live horse as Bathilde. The second was Peter Wright's version danced by Karen Kain and Frank Augustyn, with Nadia Potts as Queen of the Wilis, Hazaros Surmeyan as Hilarion, Ann Ditchburn as Bathilde, Victoria Bertram sensitively portraying Giselle's mother, and her husband, Jacques Gorrissen, playing Wilfrid, Albrecht's squire. It was taped in May 1975 and held in cans even longer than the first: it was not seen until November 1976. By that time it was rather dated and archival, since the principal artists had developed considerably.

Norman Campbell also involved us in another enjoyable project for which I provided the choreography. During the National Ballet's summer break in 1970 we danced in a TV version of Humperdinck's opera, 'Hansel and Gretel.' While it was not a National Ballet production, we did use National Ballet dancers who were happy to earn a little extra during their holidays. The cast was wonderful to work with: Judith Forst as Hansel and Christine Anton as Gretel learned their dances with alacrity and managed to dance and sing full out for cameras and microphones without bursting any blood vessels – a feat which left me speechless with admiration. One of Canada's greatest vocal treasures and ambassadresses, Maureen Forrester, kept us laughing all through rehearsals as she developed her characterization of the Witch. A large lady, Maureen, but with slender ankles; she appeared to relish doing the polka as she rode her straddled broomstick; she flew into the sky looping the loop and screeching her head off. This production was a pure delight, and it was transmitted on 23 December that year as the usual Christmas attraction; but I don't think it has been shown as often as it deserved.

The only film made of the company – an excellent documentary called 'The Looking Glass People' – was directed by Norman Campbell in March 1962. But it was for television and, after being broadcast a few times, for contractual reasons it has never been seen again. This seems especially sad since the National Film Board, with all its talent, never made a film of the company, I suspect for financial reasons.

The National Ballet has also occasionally performed for other television systems. We did a pretty show for CFTO called *Inside the National Ballet* – taped in December 1965 and shown in March 1966 with Lorne Freed as producer-director of excerpts from Kenneth MacMillan's *Solitaire* with Andrew Oxenham and Jacqueline Ivings; Ninette de

Clinton Rothwell in the title role of *Le Loup,* who becomes more beloved by the Young Bride (Veronica Tennant) as the ballet progresses. The lower photograph shows Jean-Pierre Bonnefous, a guest artist, dancing the Wolf

Valois' *The Rake's Progress* with Lois Smith; Daniel Seillier's *Rivalité* with Veronica Tennant, Lois Smith, Earl Kraul, and Lawrence Haider; *Pulcinella,* and *La Sylphide*.

In December 1955, we had been commissioned to perform live for an American system, the National Broadcasting Company. For their program 'Wide Wide World,' they wanted an episode, entitled 'The Road of North America' or some such thing, which required us to enact a backstage rehearsal with live scripted dialogue. The sequence was shot in the old Shea's theatre in Toronto, which had been closed for years. The NBC scriptwriter had written some pretty purple prose, and this I refused to accept; so their producer, our producer (Franz Kraemer), and I were locked in a hotel bedroom until the lines were changed to what I considered more acceptable to Canadian ears at that time.

Wilfred Fielding was director on that show, and he was also to be the director for a CBC show broadcast from Osaka, Japan, during Expo 1970. The National Ballet was the only classical ballet company invited to participate in the cultural activities there. In addition to our regular performances in the Festival Hall theatre, there was to be an important Canada Day celebration under the direction of Alan Lund; this was to be held in the Festival Plaza, an outdoor arena the size of two football fields, and was to be filmed for showing back home.

Patrick Reid, the commissioner general for the Canadian pavilion, had invited us to provide a few minutes of the entertainment, and the Royal Canadian Mounted Police band was to accompany us. We were to dance on a raised wooden stage constructed in the middle of the arena, so that the enormous audience, including the Emperor and Empress of Japan, could see well and so that the company would not have to dance on the dirt. I chose the waltz from

The company at Vancouver airport, en route to Osaka

the first act of *Swan Lake* (the dance performed by the Prince's friends to celebrate his twenty-first birthday) because it was lively, had colourful costumes and clean stage patterns, and was not too subtle to be viewed from a great distance and in broad daylight. Further, the music was, with a few adjustments, suitable for the band's instrumentation.

We were very excited at the prospect of taking part in the event. Alas! shortly before we left Canada for Japan we were informed that we were not to take part after all. As is often the case in diplomatic circles, no clear or satisfactory reason was given us, and it can only be supposed that those in charge thought that the *Swan Lake* waltz had to have twenty-four swans or was too patrician for the general public's taste. We were assured, however, that the decision was, of course, in the National Ballet's best interest. One will never know *who* made that decision, but it simply was not

good enough, and we did not intend to go all the way to Japan to be left out of our own country's special day. Besides, the Mounties' band had spent hours practising like fiends, and their disappointment was even greater than ours.

When we arrived at Osaka, our general manager, Wallace A. Russell, therefore did some scouting. We went to the fair grounds together and saw an attractive site right next to the Festival Plaza; it was a stone stage set in the middle of a large body of water, from which coloured fountains intermittently arose and flooded the stage. The glare from the sun and the light reflected from the water caused the dancers' faces to screw up like prunes, but the whole setting was extremely 'telegenic.' The CBC crew on the location were very much on our side and much more interested in filming the National Ballet than some of their other assignments.

After some difficulties Russell managed to hire the place; we

Mary Jago and Andrew Oxenham in
Balanchine's *Four Temperaments*

scheduled rehearsals and taping time; Lloyd Robertson and Bruno Gerussi were our extremely able CBC hosts; interpreters and Japanese camera men were hired. I had planned that the dancers (the girls were *sur les pointes*) would mark the eleven-minute waltz through on the stone stage once or twice so that the camera crew could become acquainted with the choreographic moves. Then we would go full out for the actual filming, with the fountains gushing all around; the dancers would thus only get sopping wet once, and the stone floor would only once jar their spines and bruise their toenails.

But when the dancers *did* go full out, thinking that it was 'the real thing,' the Japanese cameramen did not record after all! After two more attempts, rendered useless by communication problems with the cameramen, the dancers' union steward complained, 'Miss Franca, this is a bit much.' I was dying with worry: we had a *real* performance coming up that night at the Festival Hall theatre. But we did it once more and got it. The tape was duly inserted into the Canada Day show and I'm pleased to say it was the best thing in it.

What with the Festival Hall performances of *Romeo and Juliet*, Roland Petit's *Le Loup*, and Balanchine's *The Four Temperaments*, and what with sight-seeing in Kyoto and buying Japanese pearls, we were a tense and tired group when it was time to return home. We flew to Vancouver in a chartered plane which housed all of us along with the members of the Royal Canadian Mounted Police band. They had had a tiring schedule also. The stewards finally gave up on us and threw the bar open. I can only say that together we helped that plane fly.

# Developing Canadian Talent

In building a ballet company the commissioning of new works is of great importance. While the classic repertoire presents the ultimate challenge to principal dancers and corps de ballet alike (there can be little faking since the choreography demands and reveals all) and provides the public with the means of assessing a company's stature, the brand-new contemporary works are those which engender the most curiosity and excitement – at least among the artists and to an ever-growing extent among Canadian audiences.

We were able to produce many new ballets during our early years only because Kay Ambrose designed most of the costumes and décors for them with no remuneration other than the weekly pittance she drew as our general factotum. Talented or experienced Canadian choreographers didn't exist, since the only previous opportunities in the country to practise choreography had been with part-time regional groups.

Dancers (from whom choreographers evolve) were still learning the dance vocabulary which, technically, had been rather shakily executed for many years. Composers and designers were to a large extent unaware of the artistic opportunities ballet could provide. The National Ballet in turn had no money to offer them.

Nevertheless, it was imperative that we force the situation, and from our very first season Canadian creative artists were encouraged to produce. David Adams and Kay Armstrong were the first Canadians to choreograph for the National Ballet in its first season – without any payment, of course.

It was just as well Actors' Equity Association, the dancers' union, had not yet reared its head, for had it done so the company could not have got off the ground. While one of Equity's most loudly proclaimed complaints, when it did become active, was that dancers were subsidizing the company, it should also be remembered that, despite

Scenes from Grant Strate's *Ballad*

A scene from *Antic Spring,* a ballet by
Grant Strate about the experiences
of a country boy arriving in a big city.
The décor is by Mark Negin

Ray Powell's light and humorous *One in Five* featured one female clown (Sarah Thomas in the two larger photographs, and Jocelyn Terelle in the smallest photograph) among four male clowns (the three in the photographs are Yves Cousineau, Colin Worth, and Glenn Gilmour)

low salaries and all, they were at last given the chance to do what they most wanted to do – *dance*. If they wanted their working conditions to improve, their only chance was to devote themselves in a true pioneering spirit to the growth and development of the National Ballet.

Canadian designers were employed also during that first season: James Pape (for *Les Sylphides*), Suzanne Mess (costumes for the *Polovtsian Dances* and *Ballet behind Us*), Alan Lett (décor for the *Polovtsian Dances*), Robert Hall (décor for *The Dance of Salome*), and Gerald Budner (costumes for *The Dance of Salome*). Hector Gratton was the first composer commissioned to write an original score (*Le Pommier*); Oskar Morawetz made the reduction of *The Dance of Salome* and later in 1957 orchestrated Schumann's piano music for Fokine's ballet *Le Carnaval*.

Also in that first season Godfrey Ridout made the reduction for small orchestra of Debussy's *L'Après-midi d'un faune*. Godfrey's major contribution to the company was his excellent original score for Heino Heiden's *La Prima Ballerina*, which was created for Expo 1967 performances in Montreal. Both the score and Lawrence Schafer's costumes and décors perfectly captured the epoch of the early nineteenth century. This was an all-Canadian collaboration. Unfortunately, although Heino Heiden came up with a good scenario based on a colourful event in the life of Marie Taglioni, he had difficulty in creating the choreography. This was a pity, for he had had previous successes and received excellent reviews from no less than Paul Hume, the tough music critic of the *Washington Post*.

In 1953 George Crum persuaded Louis Applebaum, then head of music for the National Film Board and a well-known composer for Hollywood films, to write a score for *Dark of the Moon*, a new ballet by Joey Harris, born in London, Ontario. The score was very good and was used again with revisions for a second version of the ballet choreographed by David Adams in 1960 under the title of *Barbara Allen*.

A continuing problem with commissioned scorcs is the choreographer's inability to hear the full orchestration and study it by repetitive hearings before creating the dance steps. This worries many young choreographers who, on the whole, prefer to use already written and recorded music which they can listen to over and over again until they are steeped in it and, dependent upon their individual musical instincts, recognize all the nuances the score contains. I wished and wish that special arrangements could be made with the musicians' union to hire an orchestra at minimum cost to record new scores simply for study purposes. It can be argued that choreographers should learn to read a full score, but that argu-

ment is invalid, since even the composer needs to *hear* his score played before deciding what adjustments to make. If *he* can't hear it in his head, one can hardly expect that a choreographer should have that ability; in any case, his training as a dancer has probably been too time-consuming to enable him to study music in depth.

In the 1950s and 1960s it was all we could manage to have a piano score for the choreographer before rehearsals commenced with the dancers. Some of these piano scores were almost unplayable. For example, the more avant-garde Harry Somers' music became, the less he was able to notate for solo piano. He would gamely sit down at the piano and rattle off some incomprehensible stuff for *The House of Atreus*, all the while explaining that therc were wood blocks going on at this point and something else going on at that. Some of this piano score was written for four hands. Even so, as much of the first part of the ballet

Touching up the costumes for
*The House of Atreus*

was written for percussion alone, George Crum's and Harry's piano-playing consisted mostly of knocking on the wood and emitting vocal hissing sounds. Little wonder the dancers could not recognize the music when they heard it with the orchestra at that dress rehearsal!

This was really hard on the choreographer, Grant Strate, who turned out some remarkably good stuff considering the unfavourable circumstances under which he was forced to work. The dancers rehearsed with sets, costumes, and music only on the afternoon of the first performance – in Ottawa at the Capitol theatre in January 1964.

The décor and costumes were designed by a famous artist, Harold Town. The dancers were dressed basically in body tights which Harold painted with the bodies inside them. All the visible body organs were drawn and painted while the dancers stood mutely still. White eyes were depicted in strange places. Harold relished every moment; on completing someone's buttocks or genitals or breasts he would exclaim, 'Isn't that beautiful?' The paint stiffened on the tights and they were difficult to clean. The details didn't show past the first few rows in the theatre, so few were offended.

The décor, also by Town, was stunning at close quarters. Set in front of black drapes was a ramp upon which was fixed an interesting web of welded steel sections with shields stuck on them. The whole thing was designed to be taken apart or put together speedily, but we usually needed a long intermission (about half an hour) before or after a performance. The corps de ballet were supposed at one point to drape themselves around the steel pipes; but there were no braces for their feet and the dancers were uncomfortable, to put it mildly.

Before *The House of Atreus*, Harry and Grant had collaborated on two other less complex works:

Jacqueline Ivings as Clytemnestra

Characters and scenes from *The House of Atreus*, designed by Harold Town

More of *The House of Atreus.* The picture
below shows the striking set with steel
scaffolding adorned with shields

*The Remarkable Rocket,* with Hans Meister as the Remarkable Rocket and, below, David Scott as the Pyrotechnist trying to light the Rocket

*The Fisherman and His Soul*, based on Oscar Wilde's play, premiered in Hamilton in 1957; and *Ballad*, a Western with designs by Mark Negin, in 1958. As was usual in those days there were no dress rehearsals complete with orchestra, and once the ballets were premiered and into the touring repertoire there was virtually no time to make choreographic or musical revisions.

Time for creative lighting was also non-existent. Lighting plots were notated by the stage managers after consultation with the choreographers and designers, but there was no time or place to try them out. The collaborators were, not surprisingly, unhappy, but most of them understood and sympathized with our low production budgets and lack of a home theatre in which to try out effects. Our stage staff knew, however, just how much could be done in a theatre within the limitations of time and equipment.

When we presented Brian Mac-Donald's ballet *Post Script* to a Count-Basie-like jazz score by the Montreal band leader, Arthur Morrow, in Hamilton in 1956, Brian brought his own lighting designer. However, the Palace theatre in Hamilton was a cinema with a wide but shallow stage and little space in the wings for lighting towers and not enough lines to hang much equipment either. *Post Script* suffered more than was necessary because both the choreographer and the lighting designer expected more than was possible from our limited equipment and the theatre's facilities. Further, it was necessary to rehearse and perform the ballet on the same day, and the other ballets on the program also required at least a spacing rehearsal; so there was little time for re-thinking, making adjustments, or polishing details.

Poor Hamilton! Our tours were frequently started in that city, so its audiences suffered most from our lack of rehearsals in those days. Even the first North American production of the complete *Swan Lake* in four acts had its première there in a matinée performance. Three different sets of scenery, all new to the dancers, were required. The ballroom scene even had a staircase down which most of the characters entered. Lois Smith, about to dance the demanding role of Odette-Odile, had time to try out the staircase just once in her *pointe* shoes before the performance.

I can't resist recording the history of that staircase. It became known as the 'universal' because we also used it behind the scrim in *Giselle* Act II for the ghostly appearances of the Wilis. Kay knew how to stretch a penny! During a Montreal engagement at His Majesty's theatre in the fifties we opened with one program and were due to present *Giselle* later in the week. There was no room backstage to store the 'universal' and other wooden items of furniture, so we left them overnight in the filthy alley outside the stage door. Next morning, the alley was clear of everything, all having presumably been carted away by the garbage collectors! Kay spent a whole night drawing new plans on an upturned drawer in her hotel bedroom. She then managed to persuade carpenters employed by Eaton's in Montreal to build a new 'universal' in time for the performance of *Giselle*.

*The Lady from the Sea* entered our repertoire at the Carter Barron Amphitheatre, Washington, in June 1955 midway through our first historic Washington engagement. The late Elizabeth Leese was a fine modern and classical dance teacher in Montreal. She danced well herself and had choreographed several pieces for her own group, which appeared periodically in Montreal and elsewhere with the Ballet Festival Association. *The Lady from the Sea* was inspired by Ibsen's play of the same name, and Elizabeth had Montrealers Saul Honigman and Jean de Belleval write the music

Scenes from the stage productions of Erik
Bruhn's *Swan Lake:* below is the ballroom
scene; top right is the final scene with
Celia Franca as the Black Queen and Erik
Bruhn as the Prince; lower right is the
conclusion of the first lakeside scene

and design the décors respectively.

Ray Moller, a member of the company who hailed from Vancouver and who was an impressive exponent of Spanish dancing, provided us with a colourfully costumed work entitled *La Llamada (The Call)* in 1957 and a solo piece, *La Farucca*, in 1958, which was more theatrically successful. Also in the 1956–57 season David Adams' most successful and lasting divertissement entered the repertoire. *Pas de chance* was about a lady in her boudoir wooed by two suitors simultaneously. She flirts with both of them but finally accepts neither. Most of us felt that David, when he first started work on the ten-minute piece, intended to be serious, but with Angela Leigh, Ray Moller, and Harold da Silva in the cast it was interpreted by three tongues in three cheeks.

Although Ray Moller's Spanish dancing was suitably serious, his inherent sense of humour constantly came to the fore. When he first joined the company he was required to learn the role of Marvin Hudges (a bad guy) in Harris' *Barbara Allen*. I was playing the title role myself, so I told Ray the story of the ballet and explained that at a certain point in the action the crowd would lift us both high in the air; he was then to drag me down to the ground and, surrounded by the crowd, rape me. He asked, 'Is that in my contract?' At one performance, having dragged me down for the supposed rape, he asked, 'Did you bring a cheese sandwich?'

A less successful Adams ballet, *The Littlest One*, was nevertheless worthy of presentation in our 1959–60 season. John Beckwith, until recently Dean of Music at the University of Toronto, provided the music, and the costumes were designed by Cynthia MacLennan, who, together with Judy Peyton-Ward, David Pequegnat, Angela Arana, Sarah Pouliot, and a few others, is one of the rare highly skilled Canadian costume cutters

Jovial bandits in *La Prima Ballerina:* left,
Glenn Gilmour and Lawrence Adams;
right, Howard Marcus on the back of
Andrew Oxenham

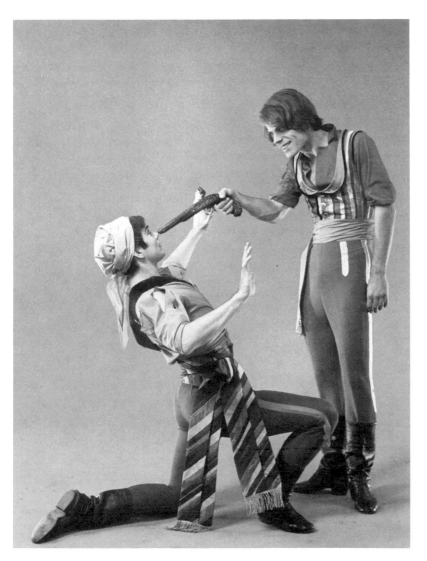

Gilmour and Adams spoof it up again in
the studio

so much sought after by designers from distant parts of the world.

During this same season David created the lovely *Pas de deux romantique* for himself and Lois. The choreography was in the style of the Bolshoi Ballet with its spectacular lifts and was difficult to rehearse. David and Lois had some tense moments over it, but it turned out to be a very personal statement; at their request it was never danced by another couple.

The 1960–61 season brought two more new ballets by Canadian choreographers. Grant Strate, our resident choreographer, collaborated again with designer Mark Negin for *Antic Spring*, a charming and useful work about a young country boy's experience in a big city. I was grateful for a jolly ballet with which we could open or close a program. It was a pity we had to drop this work from the repertoire after a while; the royalties on Jacques Ibert's music were too steep for us at that time.

That same season, a vital Canadian dancer-choreographer named Don Gillies, who had danced with the Sadler's Wells Theatre Ballet in England before returning home to Toronto to choreograph for television, created *The Remarkable Rocket* for us. The scenario, adapted from Oscar Wilde's delightful story about a beautiful princess and a firework display, gave opportunities for lively dances. Don had bad luck with the ballet. He had wanted Phil Nimmons to write the score, but Phil had to back out at the last minute. George Crum knew that Morris Surdin could compose very quickly, so we prevailed upon the already overworked film and radio composer to save the day. Once I phoned Morris to see how he was progressing with the score; he sang parts of what he had finished while simultaneously writing new music. Jack Nichols, one of Canada's fine painters, agreed to design the décor and costumes, but we were unable to do justice to the scenic design because it was

The two top photographs are of Kenneth MacMillan's *Solitaire*, showing the Boys' dance. Below, Lois Smith and Earl Kraul in the slow movement of *Triptych*

*Pulcinella,* choreographed by Grant Strate
and designed by Mark Negin

For *The Rake's Progress*, Lawrence Schafer reproduced Rex Whistler's sets inspired by Hogarth's prints – as indeed was the whole ballet. Lawrence Adams is the Rake below, and Jeremy Blanton the Rake in the orgy scene, below right. Above, from left to right, are the Rake's debtors being placated by the Betrayed Girl (Lois Smith), the final scene with the Rake in the Mad House, and Lois Smith in the sewing dance

executed too cheaply and we had insufficient time on the Royal Alexandra stage to set it up and light it properly. The costumes, on the other hand, were executed marvellously in our own wardrobe department with Sarah Pouliot as principal cutter. Although the ballet had some excellent theatrical moments, it just did not gel. The costumes were lovingly preserved for posterity by Jimmy Ronaldson, but they were destroyed together with those for *Romeo and Juliet* and many other ballets by the fire which broke out in our storage room at the St Lawrence Hall on 1 October 1973.

Grant Strate did two ballets for the Stratford Music Festival, ingeniously using the famous thrust stage with its side staircases and pillar-supported balcony envisioned by Tyrone Guthrie and designed by Tanya Moiseiwitsch. The first ballet, in 1962, was *Time Cycle*, with costumes again by Mark Negin. The second, in 1964, was *Electre,* Grant's third essay on this theme (the first being a sketch for *The House of Atreus* choreographed for the Juilliard School of Music in New York while Grant was on leave of absence, and the second being *The House of Atreus* itself).

*Triptych*, so titled because Mozart's clarinet concerto is in three movements, was a practical and inexpensive Strate ballet. An abstract work requiring no scenery and the simplest of costumes, it was easy to tour. However, his next ballet, *Pulcinella*, to Stravinsky's music and Negin's designs, was more elaborate and unfortunately less successful. It was premiered at Montreal's Place des Arts in November 1965. Grant himself asked me to take it out of the repertoire.

In 1964 we made the move in Toronto from the Royal Alexandra theatre to the much larger stage, pit, and auditorium of the O'Keefe centre. The move was made in April 1964 after much deliberation by all the parties involved. The larger theatre meant greater expenditures; more expensive promotion to help fill the 3200 seats; more massive scenery; more elaborate costumes; and a full-size symphony orchestra to accommodate irreducible scores like Prokofiev's *Romeo and Juliet* and *Cinderella.* At last, George Crum could have his big orchestra.

The timing of the move and the size of the new theatre created severe problems. Our classical productions, besides being too small in scale for the O'Keefe stage, were worn out; even if we had stayed at the Royal Alex we would have had to redesign and remake the décor and costumes. Audiences were beginning to expect higher standards of production; labour and production costs were increasing too, but our income and grants could not cover the costs of rebuilding our repertoire virtually from scratch. It was like starting all over again thirteen years later.

Popular one-act works like *Offenbach in the Underworld* and *Pineapple Poll* had one more season in the O'Keefe theatre, looking ludicrously under-scaled on the large stage. We had also to drop our *Coppélia* completely, but our *Swan Lake* struggled on for a while in a bedraggled fashion. So did *Les Sylphides,* despite the archetypal problem of our old drops hanging too short and narrow at the back of the stage. We had to surround them with black drapes and close in the top and sides of the proscenium, with the result that the view for members of the audience sitting at the sides was not what it should have been. I felt very ashamed.

We had foreseen these difficulties about the move, however, but I felt also that the time had come for the dancers to stretch their lungs and legs. The National Ballet School had been training students to dance with broad movements, and Betty Oliphant's first graduates were ready to become professionals. Though the quality of our costumes and décor was poor, at least the dancers were provided with the opportunity and challenge, which some of them were admittedly not very happy about, of broadening their physical style and powers of projection.

We expected too that other larger theatres were about to be built elsewhere in the country, so we took the risk and tried to start adjusting to this new expensive style of production. But we could not begin to plan large-scale works only, and in the spring season for 1964 we tended to present ballets which required no décor other than a skycloth: Zachary Solov's *Allégresse,* an abstract work in neo-classic style danced to Mendelssohn's first piano concerto; Balanchine's *Serenade* and *Concerto Barocco;* and Ray Powell's *One in Five,* which was never intended for a large stage but came across remarkably well. Programs were filled out with various pas de deux from *Sleeping Beauty, Le Corsair,* and *Walpurgis Night.* Our

major Canadian work that season, *The House of Atreus,* unfortunately did not carry as well in the O'Keefe theatre as it had in the smaller Capitol in Ottawa.

The 1964 season was saved, however, by our large-scale production of *Romeo and Juliet,* with its inspired choreography by John Cranko, glorious music by Serge Prokofiev, and magnificent décors and costumes designed by Jürgen Rose. Galina Samtsova and Earl Kraul were to dance the leading roles on the opening night – at the Place des Arts in Montreal – but Galina sprained an ankle and our guest stars from the Stuttgart Ballet, Marcia Haydée and Ray Barra, took over. Audiences and critics alike were ecstatic, and a week later Toronto was equally bowled over by the performances in the O'Keefe theatre.

It was by sheer good fortune that we obtained this ballet. Whenever Grant Strate went to Europe on holiday or sabbatical, he would act as a talent scout. He would audition

A group from *Solitaire*

any European dancers who had applied for positions with us, and he would look out for new ballets that might suit our company. We were still at this time not able to employ the dancers for a whole year, but we did manage to pay a small retainer to some principals, so Grant was able to go abroad fairly regularly.

During one of his trips in Europe, I received a letter from him in Stuttgart, full of enthusiasm for Cranko's new ballet which he had just seen. He thought our company could do it well, and I wrote back asking for details so that I could estimate the costs. How many painted drops? Properties? How many costumes? He sent back a house program so that I could see a list of characters; but the citizens, soldiers, pages, and peasants were not enumerated and I had to guess what the cost would be. Twenty thousand dollars – in those days a huge amount of money for us!

I happened to have known John Cranko, however, when he came to London from South Africa to join the Sadler's Wells Theatre Ballet and, years later, Grant and I had gone to London to learn *Pineapple Poll* from him in his flat. John was willing to come to Canada with Jürgen Rose to put on *Romeo and Juliet.* This was exactly the kind of production we needed – important and sure-fire – to allay the fears about our moving into larger theatres. I was determined to add it to our repertoire.

With some trepidation I sent off a telegram to our general manager, Carman Guild, then on holiday beyond the reach of telephones in Georgian Bay, asking if we could proceed. Carman thought that, despite the risk, it was a responsible decision; I could go ahead. The National Ballet should be eternally grateful to him for that decision; it allowed us to make the leap into full-length, top-quality, large-scale work.

It turned out, when Cranko and Rose arrived with their designs, that I had underestimated the number of costumes and properties required. The staging of *Romeo and Juliet* eventually cost us more than three times my original budget; but it was still cheap at the price! The success of this production took us over an important hurdle – artistic, psychological, financial – though, of course, the race went on and we continued developing work by Canadian choreographers.

Indeed, during the 1960s I began to experience increasing pressure on me to present such new works. It seemed to be imagined that they would be instant box-office successes and could be produced for next to nothing – this despite the fact that what we had already presented did not command a constant following and in Canada generally there were no choreographers creating great new works. The promising young choreographers of today, like Ann Ditchburn and James Kudelka, had not yet graduated from the school.

In 1967, for example, it was considered important – and rightly so – that the National Ballet participate in the cultural activities at Montreal's Expo. But I was led to believe that if we did not produce a specially created Canadian ballet, we would not be allowed to perform at all. So we presented *La Prima Ballerina,* with choreography by Heino Heiden to music by Godfrey Ridout and designs by Lawrence Schafer. This work also served as a needed vehicle for Lois Smith, who danced the leading role. The ballet told the story of how Marie Taglioni was once captured by some jolly bandits.

Soon afterwards Ann Ditchburn, Tim Spain, and David Gordon joined the company and increased the demand for Canadian choreography. This 'rebellious trio' was supported by some dancers 'bored' with the classics and others who found them difficult to perform and were looking for different outlets. There was a movement to revolutionize the repertoire, so I responded by opening our 1971

Photographs of the twenty-fifth anniversary season's production of *Romeo and Juliet*. Right, Lady Capulet brings the ball dress to Juliet in the garden; below left, Romeo pulls himself up for a final kiss in the balcony scene; below right, the bedroom scene

The brawl between the Montagues and
the Capulets from the first scene

Earl Kraul in a tap dance from *Eh!*

season at the O'Keefe with a mixed program of new works. It was a gamble and I lost.

Ann Ditchburn and Tim Spain had both created promising works at the School's workshops, so we included works by them. Ann's *Brown Earth*, with songs by Laura Nyro and designs by Jack King, made a real effort to appeal to audiences, but the choreography came across as rather thin. Ann was disappointed herself when she watched the work from the back of the auditorium, but she had the courage to try again. Her *Kisses*, first created in England at a Royal Ballet workshop and added to our repertoire in 1975, was a slight but entertaining ballet which won public acceptance. Then her all-Canadian *Mad Shadows*, first produced in 1977 and based on Marie-Claire Blais' novel 'La Belle Bête' with music by André Gagnon and designs by Jack King, was successful enough that the company performed it the next year in the Metropolitan Opera House in New York.

Tim Spain had constructed a refreshing pas de deux for himself and Karen Kain, danced to music by Padre Antonio Soler, but his two works that we presented that season – *For Internal Use as Well*, a pas de trois to music by John Mills-Cockell, and *Sagar*, an idealistic 'togetherness' ballet with pleasant electronic music by Morton Subotnick – were too esoteric for the public. His works were generally introspective, and he became discouraged and left Canada after a while to join the London Festival Ballet after our first European tour.

Amid these ups and downs, however, we should recall that in the 1968–69 season we presented two ballets that were probably the best works Grant Strate ever produced for the National Ballet. They were *Phases*, a pas de deux to Eric Satie's 'Gymnopédies,' which was equally successful on large or small stages, and *Cyclus*, a ballet in four movements – Peace, Conflict, Victory, and Reconstruction.

*Sagar,* choreographed by Timothy Spain. Shown below are Tomas Schramek and Ann Ditchburn

*Cyclus* was an anti-war ballet by
Grant Strate

*Cyclus*

The latter work was choreographed while Grant was on leave of absence in Antwerp, and the music and design were done by Belgians, Peter Welffens and John Bogaerts.

Grant also created *The Arena* for our Ballet Concert, which Bogaerts also designed, though he painted Nadia Potts' body tights in what struck me as a distasteful fashion. Chamber ballets had long been an ambition of mine and in 1967 we established such a ballet company under the title Ballet Concert. The idea behind it was that we could not take the whole company to smaller towns with at best a modest high school auditorium, but that we could send a smaller company of around eighteen dancers, twelve musicians, and a simple portable set suitable for all the ballets performed. We commissioned choreography to be danced with chamber music and in small theatres; interesting new – and inexpensive – works were created by Strate and by Heinz Poll, now artistic director of the

Ohio Ballet; I did a couple myself, and David Gordon received an opportunity to choreograph a pas de deux for Veronica Tennant and himself.

It was a grant from the Ontario Arts Council for Centennial Year celebrations that allowed us to launch our Ballet Concert, but the special OAC grant was only to help us start up and we eventually had to drop the program. At its peak, when it was still not possible to offer a full year's employment to the dancers and staff of the company, we would divide the company at times into three separate groups – two groups of the Ballet Concert, one touring Ontario and the other western Canada, and a smaller group of dancers with only a piano and tapes for accompaniment, which worked with Prologue to the Performing Arts, an Ontario program which presented 'mini' plays, operas, and ballets to the schools.

I was very sorry when we had to discontinue these activities in

Another scene from *Cyclus*

1971. Not only were we providing work for the company, but we were building up audiences and we were providing opportunities for new and experimental choreography. I had hoped to be able to commission new music as well for such productions, but these prospects came to naught. The parent company, however, used some of these ballets when it had to perform on small stages, so all was not lost.

In 1974 we premiered the last new ballets that might be mentioned here. The first was *Whispers of Darkness,* set to music by Gustav Mahler by Norbert Vesak, a Canadian choreographer who had worked mostly in the United States but had also produced for the Royal Winnipeg Ballet two works, *The Ecstasy of Rita Joe* and *Wait until the Messiah Comes,* which achieved a considerable success. He wanted to create a ballet for our well-trained classical dancers, and I thought it only fair that he should have the chance. Norbert asked the well-known

New York stage designer, Ming Cho Lee, to provide the décor; but effective as the modern abstract structure was, it was diametrically opposed to the romantic music and the choreography. Norbert's costume designs were also rather unsuitable, and there was nothing we could do to salvage what could have been a good ballet.

On the same night – 2 October 1974, in Quebec City – we also premiered two other new ballets: Gerald Arpino's *Kettentanz* and Constantin Patsalas' *Inventions.* It was, of course, a kind of madness to present three new works at the same time, but it was unavoidable because of our lack of a home theatre where new ballets could be tried out as they were ready. And once on the road – this performance at Quebec City was the start of a five-week tour – there was no time or place for rehearsals or revisions. Unlike Broadway musicals which have long periods on the road with ample time for revisions before presentation in

Peter Wright's *Mirror Walkers*, with
Clinton Rothwell and Mary Jago in black,
and Karen Kain and Jeremy Blanton in
white

the 'Big Apple,' our ballets were unalterable once we had started our touring circuits.

Arpino was a guest choreographer from the Joffrey Ballet in the States, and Patsalas was a member of our own company. His ballet had the least stage rehearsal of the three, but Constantin's lighting plot was extemely complicated; in the actual first performance, almost every cue was late. His ballets, *Inventions* and *Black Angels,* presented a few years later, remain to my taste the most interesting of the company's Canadian works, and I look forward to his new works with the greatest curiosity.

When I look back on all the works that have been created in this country, however, I have to admit that most of them have not warranted a permanent place in the repertoire. It would have been miraculous, of course, if things were otherwise, since the choreographers and other artists had no established theatrical tradition to guide, nourish, and inspire them. What is important is rather that much was attempted and that there were some ballets created which happily survived several seasons – and may even one day be revived.

# The National Ballet School

When I came to Canada in 1951, Betty Oliphant was supporting herself and her two children, Gail and Carol, by teaching ballet and tap-dancing, and even at times acrobatic and ballroom dancing, at 444 Sherbourne Street in Toronto. She had received her dance training in England, where she obtained her certificates from the Imperial Society of Teachers of Dancing in the Stage, Ballroom, and Classical Ballet (Cecchetti) Branches. At the tender age of eighteen, she had opened her own studio on Wigmore Street in London when she realized that she was growing too tall to dance professionally. She married a Canadian and came to Canada in 1947, but her husband left her soon afterwards.

Betty was not only a born organizer – she was a founder and member of the executive committee of the Canadian Dance Teachers Association – but also a very fine teacher. I asked her, as the only qualified member of the Cecchetti syllabi, to join me in my first summer school; this she did, at the cost of giving up her own. She was caught up in the excitement of future prospects and threw herself wholeheartedly into the work of the school. In 1952 she became the company's ballet mistress, albeit on a part-time basis so that she could keep her own school going.

At first I taught most of the company classes myself in order to encourage the dancers to look professional and help them absorb long combinations of dance steps as exercises for learning and retaining ballets. It was important too to stimulate their imaginations so that they could understand and interpret choreographic direction. But it also became clear that we would have to 'break down' the dancers' techniques and have them understand and practise basics. This difficult task fell to Betty and for a while the dancers were not keen about being put through exercises that seemed boring and elementary. But we both knew that

Betty Oliphant leads a 1955 class of future ballerinas in her school at 444 Sherbourne Street, Toronto. From left to right in the front row are Nadia Potts, Vanessa Harwood, and Linda Fletcher; in the second row, Victoria Bertram, Barbara Malinowski, and Linda Stibbard; in the back row, Carol Oliphant, Janet Battye, and Veronica Tennant

for the long term such a training policy was essential, and to give evidence of our belief we decided that I should teach basic classes myself at future summer schools.

My own training had been under the auspices of the Royal Academy of Dancing, a body also well established in Canada. I had passed the advanced RAD exam when I was thirteen, but I had been a pupil of Stanislas Idzikowski, one of Enrico Cecchetti's favourite pupils. So, to encourage dancers and teachers to appreciate the Cecchetti syllabi and because Betty as Cecchetti secretary for Canada needed qualified examiners, at the age of thirty I tried for the elementary and intermediate tests of the Cecchetti Major Examinations. Betty patiently coached me, and I just scraped through.

We became very good friends, Betty and I; for a long time I was 'Auntie Celia' to her children, now grown up with children of their own. As the reputation of the summer school in the St Lawrence Hall grew and as attendance from all over Canada and the United States increased, we worked harder and harder. Classes began early in the morning, and we had evening sessions as well. Before these, Betty and I would sometimes refresh ourselves with Manhattans at Letros, a tavern a few minutes walk along King Street. One particularly hot and humid evening, Betty and I floated back to the school, where it was my turn to teach the 'babies' class under the eyes of their parents. Betty tried to stifle her giggles as I staggered to place the portable *barres* in the middle of the classroom and she continued laughing as I taught, as best I could, the most complicated polka step imaginable!

However, company classes and summer schools could only be a beginning. All along, I knew that if the National Ballet was to become a permanent institution we would have to establish a residential school in which we could house

Grant Strate conducts one of his ballets with Timothy Spain and Karen Bowes (also on the left). Watching are Alastair Munro, Earl Kraul, and Anthony Clarke, then stage manager, who is operating the tape recorder

Ann Ditchburn choreographs a
solo for Louise Kent in 'An Evening of
Contemporary Dance' presented at the
Edward Johnson Building in Toronto

talented young students and also
provide them with a well-rounded
academic and artistic education.
Only in this way could the continuity of the company be ensured
and only in this way could it rely
on its new members having an
adequate and standard training.
There was no great future in trying
to reform and patch up students'
skills for two months each
summer, or in company classes.

At this time promising children
were going to Betty Oliphant's
studio after academic school
hours. Lorna Geddes from Kitchener and Charmain Turner from
London made the terrific effort of
travelling to Toronto at weekends.
Among the other children then
attending 444 Sherbourne Street
were Victoria Bertram, Vanessa
Harwood, Barbara Malinowski,
Nadia Potts, and Veronica Tennant.
I was most anxious that they and
other youngsters have the benefit
of a regular timetable and an enrich-
ed dance program. The next generation of dancers had to be better.

I had a lot of talking to do. Our
directors could barely raise enough
funds to keep the company alive,
far less take on the burden of a
private school. Fortunately,
however, several board members
were interested in education. Particularly enthusiastic was Eddie
Goodman, who arranged meetings
with such people as John Robarts,
then minister of education in
Ontario, to gain moral support. At
one board meeting, when Eddie
said that he would like to start a
project to raise money for the
school and other members
objected, he retorted with 'What
are you going to do? Impeach me?'

When the idea of the school
seemed eventually to be generally
accepted among the board members, they met in Eddie Goodman's
office. For reasons best known to
himself, Arthur Gelber began to
provoke me; my nerves would take
no more and I shouted out, 'Don't
you trust me yet after all these
years?' Goodman, in the chair as
president, told me that if I didn't

Young hopefuls

A selection of studio photographs. Right, Lois Smith in flight; below left, three soloists from *Bayaderka* – Mary Jago, Vanessa Harwood, and Maureen Rothwell; below right, a group of National Ballet 'beauties' – Karen Bowes (top), Nadia Potts, Vanessa Harwood, and Leeyan Granger (sitting on the floor). Opposite top: Angelica Bornhausen and Hazaros Surmeyan in a 'fish'; below, Karen Bowes (left) and Veronica Tennant (right) in a romantic pose

like my board I could go out and get another one. The worst part about my tears was that I didn't have enough Kleenex. But the school was approved.

In 1958 Mrs Elsie Agnew and Miss Mildred Wickson (as the first president of the Canadian Dance Teachers Association, Millie gave me her utmost support for many years) found a church building in Toronto at 111 Maitland Street. This became our main school, and a house around the corner at 410 Jarvis Street was to serve as our first residence. John Osler of the board was asked to acquire the buildings, and he also sat down with Betty to interview and hire the academic staff.

Betty, of course, became principal of the National Ballet School and so gave up her own school. The new ballet teachers had all previously taught at the summer schools – Nancy Schwenker, Juliette Fisher, and Lucille McClure. The academic staff was headed by Anna Haworth. Betty's

students and some children from out of town who had regularly attended our summer schools made up the student body that first year: fifteen students lived in the residence and twelve came for the day; there were no male students, but it did not take long for that to change. There was also a Ballet Division to teach children who came only after their regular school hours; two hundred and thirty were enrolled when the school started and their fees were important for many years in keeping the school in financial health.

The school has been a great success. This year (1977-78) the enrolment is 35 boys and 82 girls, along with 13 boys and 18 girls in the Special Ballet Division which teaches graduates and student teachers. Betty Oliphant, now director and principal, and vice-principal Carole Chadwick are assisted by 14 ballet teachers; Mrs Lucy Potts heads an academic staff of 15, and there is a support staff of 34. The school now occupies seven

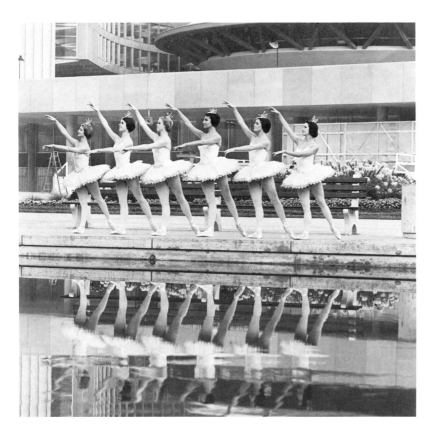

Company publicity shots for souvenir programs, showing the dancers at Toronto city hall and the Royal Ontario Museum

buildings, containing dance studios, academic classrooms, and residential accommodation. It has long been run by its own board of directors, to avoid confusion about fund-raising, but some members of the board of the ballet company have also always been part of the school board and *vice versa.* Under Betty's skilled direction, the school has become one of the finest in the world, as its many lovely dancers gracing the stages of Canada and other countries have amply proved.

# International Affairs

There were many times when it seemed, despite all we managed to accomplish, that the company's progress towards international standards was frustratingly slow. These frustrations were not mine alone – they were also voiced by critics, directors, and members of grant-giving bodies, and they could be not very friendly. When the company would be feeling 'down' and looking for some tender loving care and understanding, that, of course, would be the moment when the Toronto critics thrust their daggers in more viciously than usual.

One such time occurred around 1960, and as a result it gave the members of the Canada Council several cold feet. The council had formed in 1957 to support and develop all kinds of cultural activities, and the National Ballet, in some ways the prototype of institutions like the Stratford Festival or the Canadian Opera Company, was given an annual grant. In 1960, when we hoped for perhaps more assistance, they spent money inviting 'experts' from other countries to observe and assess what we were doing. Their report was devastating, apparently, and it was never distributed. Our general manager was invited to read it, provided he didn't show it to me; he declined. There was even a rumour that the company might receive $100 000 if it obtained the services of an artistic director other than myself!

This kind of situation was not one the company could long live with. We needed to know where we stood with the Canada Council before going out to raise money or deal with our creditors; without some assurance from the Council we would be in a weak position in asking for private donations. And money or credit was needed to start work on the next season.

Our board and representatives of the Canada Council negotiated. 'Well, gentlemen,' our directors asked, 'do you want a ballet company?' After a thoughtful pause,

Madge the Witch warms herself by the fire in the first act of *La Sylphide.* Below, Lois Smith as the Sylphide and Earl Kraul as James, flaunting the fatal scarf

*La Sylphide.* Right, the girls ask James
(Earl Kraul) to let Madge the Witch tell
their fortunes; below, Lois Smith as the
Sylphide is about to waken James with
a kiss; and Smith and Kraul in the second
act. Opposite: top, Rebecca Bryan as
Effie and Rudolf Nureyev as James;
below, Joysanne Sidimus as a sylph,
and Earl Kraul as James

they got the answer, 'Well, I think not.' But that cleared the air; all got down to business and settled the matter; we got our grant.

It is hard to believe some of the financial straits we were in. Once Carman Guild had bought his wife an electric blanket, but something was urgently needed for the ballet, so he whipped it off the bed and returned it to Eaton's for cash – which he gave us. Our comptroller, Nora Woods, was jolly and rotund and skilled in handling creditors. But sometimes their phone calls got through to the company manager, Robert Osborne, who would tell them, 'Mrs Woods has just jumped out of the window. I'll see if I can catch her on the way down,' or 'She just ran round the corner with a rat in her mouth.'

Once Antony Tudor threatened to complain to the American Guild of Musical Artists about our not paying him royalties of his productions. He had asked for the money to be kept in our account – where it was soon spent by the broke company. Eddie Goodman somehow managed to solve that problem.

This hand-to-mouth existence in a country with few good theatres was not such as to encourage us to invite choreographers or dancers of international reputation, or to encourage them to accept. Canada lay like a wilderness between Europe and the United States, without adequate stages, lighting, rehearsals, or dollars. We were certainly not in a position, during the fifties and early sixties, to invite a Margot Fonteyn to dance with us.

The National Ballet was fortunate, however, in being able to get rights to perform many works by British choreographers such as Tudor, Andrée Howard, and Frederick Ashton. This was largely owing to my acquaintance and friendship with colleagues in the Ballet Rambert and the Sadler's Wells companies from my earlier days in London. These choreographers were paid, of course, but not richly.

It was not until 1963 that we invited a guest artist to come and dance with the company. It was a rough experience, as it turned out. Lois Smith was injured, so we decided to invite Melissa Hayden, then a Canadian-born principal dancer with Balanchine's New York City Centre Ballet. An obvious choice. She accepted at once, attracted by the opportunity of dancing the full-length classics, *Swan Lake* and *Coppélia.* It seemed natural to ask her to appear also in Balanchine's *Concerto Barocco* and *Serenade* – ballets that had been admirably staged for us by Una Kai, one of Balanchine's *répétiteurs.*

I went to New York to teach Miss Hayden the role of Swanilda, and in February 1963 she joined the company in Windsor, where we were performing, in order to rehearse with the whole company. After our four-week season at the Royal Alex we were nervous wrecks; we had had enough. She made last-minute changes to the Balanchine ballets, which made her look splendid and our own dancers inept; she refused to dance with Earl Kraul, so David Adams had to partner her throughout. He said he would never go through that again (and I told him I wouldn't expect it); Miss Hayden would become very nervous in the classics, forget the choreography, and blame David for the mistakes. David is one of the strongest and most reliable partners anyone could wish for, but he never knew where she was going on stage.

The critics were delighted by Miss Hayden's performances, which they said showed up the incompetence of the other dancers. It is easy and indeed right to sympathize with guest artists who suffer from nerves because they know all eyes are upon them, but it is another matter when they put down their fellow dancers. Perhaps, ultimately, Millie was scared by the demands of the classic ballets and could not help taking it out on our vulnerable

222

Scenes from a 1967 presentation of the new *Swan Lake*, choreographed by Erik Bruhn in two acts

little company. Anyhow, I decided that we were better off, even at a time when we could not afford understudies, managing with our own limited resources.

Melissa Hayden was a well established and popular dancer, and the problem was not all hers. Different companies have different styles and disciplines, and harmony between guest 'stars' and a company is not always achieved. On the whole, however, most of the guest artists the company has invited since then have been a pleasure to work with.

Erik Bruhn was invited to Toronto to produce *La Sylphide* towards the end of 1964. He was going to dance James himself, we had enjoyed rehearsing with him, and we were looking forward with great excitement to our first gala performance on 31 December. In the midst of this excitement, there was more: Rudolf Nureyev, on a two-week holiday from the Royal Ballet in London, flew across to see his friend's new production. This

news spread like wildfire, and Nureyev was surrounded by photographers, reporters, and TV cameras. He watched the premiere, in which Erik danced marvelously, Lynn Seymour was charmingly plump in the title role, and the company supported them in fine style. Backstage afterwards, Rudi tugged at my hair which showed under my Witch's cap, saying 'You were very good. Perhaps more hair higher. Is suggestion only.'

Erik danced again the next night, though he was complaining of a sore knee. I had suspected that Nureyev had come to Toronto because he wanted to add *La Sylphide* to his repertoire, and, after consulting with Erik, I invited him to dance the third performance. He wanted to rehearse with the whole company, which meant expensive overtime; when it was all organized he and Bruhn didn't turn up. Then he slipped on an icy street and sprained both ankles. But on 5 January he went on stage and

More of *Swan Lake*: Yves Cousineau
and Hazaros Surmeyan as the Prince;
Surmeyan with Martine van Hamel as
Odette/Odile; Celia Franca as the Black
Queen haunts the principals; Earl Kraul
and Lois Smith also played the leading
roles; a group from the first scene.
Opposite are two moments from the first
lakeside scene when the Prince
encounters Odette and the Swan Maidens

danced the role; Rudi had tremendous physical courage.

In *Swan Lake* on one occasion, a guest artist from the New York City Center Ballet, Suzanne Farrell, twisted her knee while executing the famous fouettés rond de jambe en tournant in the ballroom scene and she had to hobble off stage. After the fouettés there are still several minutes of music before the scene ends; in Bruhn's *Swan Lake* there is no curtain or intermission at this point and the backdrops are flown in and out and the thrones removed during a minute or so of semi-darkness. I was playing the Queen Mother that night, sitting on one of the thrones; to fill out the music and bring the scene to an end, I descended from the throne and smilingly muttered to the ball guests to follow me round the stage in a grande promenade. We all got into formation and marched round the stage, but I couldn't understand why the girls wore such sickly expressions on their faces and

seemed to be twisting round to face the audience. And then I noticed: they had all undone the hooks on the backs of their costumes in order to speed up their quick change into swans for the final scene by the lakeside, and they were embarrassed about displaying a little nudity.

The curtain came down, George Crum stopped the orchestra, an announcement was made, and Nadia Potts was hastily taught the last scene by Hazaros Surmeyan, the Prince, and ballet masters Joanne Nisbet and David Scott. This was Nadia's début as the Swan Queen. She went on to dance the complete role in Montreal in September 1975 when her Prince was one of the most distinguished, well-mannered, unselfish, and supportive of our guest artists – Mikhail Baryshnikov.

Baryshnikov had slipped away in a waiting car after performing in Toronto with a section of the Bolshoi Ballet. When he came out of seclusion, he took classes with

Mikhail Baryshnikov

*The Nutcracker.* The Sugar Plum Fairy enters the Kingdom of Sweets, populated by students from the National Ballet School

*The Nutcracker* snow scene, with the
Snowmen dancing with Clara and the
Snow Maidens

Martine van Hamel in a variation from
*Le Corsair*

our company and rehearsed the role of James in *La Sylphide.* This he danced with us in a not very artistic version for CBC television and again in the Forum at Ontario Place before some ten thousand enthralled people.

While we were thus improving our ability to attract guest dancers and choreographers, we were also thinking about the other side of international relations – being seen and known outside Canada and the United States. We had made only one visit to another country in our earlier days – to Mexico City in 1958. Lois, David, Earl, Angela, Lilian, Judy, Grant, and many of the original gang were still together and we did our best, when not suffering from Montezuma's revenge, to survive twenty-six performances in twenty-two days.

This schedule was very hard-going, for we had not reckoned on the extra effort needed to dance at the high altitude of Mexico City. We took a large repertoire there, including demanding and indeed

exhausting classics and shorter works. At the end of one performance of *Winter Night,* when I had to be on stage for thirty minutes with only a one-minute break in the wings, I knelt down to curtsey and just kept on going. I came to in the arms of two huge firemen – they were stationed in the wings to administer oxygen – as they carried me to my dressing room, followed by an anxious Kay.

We were invited back to Mexico City in 1968 as part of the cultural side to the Olympic Games. We had a lot of new talented dancers from the school and elsewhere with us this time – Veronica Tennant, Lawrence Adams, Howard Marcus, Andrew Oxenham, Karen Bowes, Hazaros Surmeyan, Peter Schaufuss, Jeremy Blanton, Nadia Potts, Mary Jago, Clinton Rothwell, Vanessa Harwood, and Martine van Hamel. We performed *Romeo and Juliet,* Bruhn's *Swan Lake* and *La Sylphide,* my 1964 production of *The Nutcracker* (called by one reviewer 'wall-to-wall splendour'), Kenneth MacMillan's *Solitaire, Concerto Barocco,* and the pas de deux from *Le Corsair* and *Don Quixote.*

Taking the entire company overseas was a costly way of achieving some international recognition, but there was another cheaper way. In the summer of 1966 a small group from the company had gone to the International Ballet Competition at Varna, Bulgaria. The Canada Council and the Laidlaw Foundation paid for the trip, and George MacPherson, our publicity director, arranged VIP treatment for us on Air India. Betty Oliphant and I agreed that Martine van Hamel stood a good chance of winning a medal, and I thought that we should also ask Karen Bowes, although she had not yet graduated from the school, to participate in the competition for the sake of experience and observing the work of dancers from different parts of the world. Earl Kraul and Alastair Munro came along as non-competing partners for Martine

and Karen respectively, and Mary McDonald was our pianist.

Both girls were entered in the junior class, and both passed the preliminary round. Karen didn't get past the semi-finals, but everyone liked her lyrical style. To our delight, Martine astonished jury and audience alike and won a gold medal and a special prize for artistic interpretation. (Mikhail Baryshnikov won the Competition's junior gold medal for a male dancer that year.) There was now some evidence in the 'ballet world' that Canada existed and could boast a little culture.

Martine danced the pas de deux and variations from *Le Corsair* for the preliminary round. Earl Kraul partnered her marvellously, and I was so glad that they danced Galina Samtsova's version which she had learned in Kiev before marrying a Canadian, Alex Ursuliak, and coming to this country. I still think it the best version I have seen, and it was one of my favourites to coach. For the second

Martine van Hamel and Earl Kraul in her prize-winning pas de deux from *Le Corsair*

round, Martine danced the pas de deux (with Earl) from *Solitaire* and the First Song from *Dark Elegies.* In the final round she and Earl performed a pas de deux and other excerpts from *Bayaderka,* a work which had just been taught us in Toronto by a guest teacher, Eugen Valukin from the Bolshoi Ballet. When we returned to Canada, Valukin was as proud and happy at Martine's triumph as any of our Canadian friends. George Mac-Pherson organized a ticker-tape parade down Bay Street in Toronto, but it has to be admitted that most people did not recognize what an important success this was for the country.

1970 was a leaner year and we had to reduce the number of dancers, but some of us went off to Varna again. I was on the jury, and Nadia Potts and Clinton Rothwell agreed to compete. The company would look after everything for the dancers and they did not need to worry about costumes, music, accompaniment, rehearsal costs,

and so on, as many other competitors did. I was even given samples of coloured gelatins and lighting instructions from our stage managers, but if a candidate looked promising the stage at Varna was flooded automatically in bright white light for the sake of television cameras. Nadia won a bronze medal, and Clinton received the highest points for his *Le Loup* in the second round but his classical work held him back. He and Nadia also carried off a prize for the best duet.

In 1972, thanks to a grant from the Department of External Affairs, the company was at last able, as it was also ready, to undertake something I had felt it should some day do – we went off on our first European tour. It was cause for celebration, but it was also a cause for some nerves on my part. We were to open at the Coliseum theatre in London on 17 May, and my former teachers and colleagues would surely attend. What would they think of what I had to show

Left, the pas de deux from the ballroom scene in *Cinderella*; Veronica Tennant is Cinderella and Jeremy Blanton is Prince Charming. Below, the apotheosis, when Cinderella (Nadia Potts) and her Prince (Hazaros Surmeyan), attended by the Fairies of the Four Seasons, the Fairy Godmother, and baby fairies from the National Ballet School, begin to live happily ever after

after twenty-two years?

I flew over a week early to do some advance publicity. I spoke to a meeting of the London Ballet Circle, and I faced an army of reporters in Canada House. Belle Shenkman, a Canadian living in London, was in charge of our opening night, which was to be a gala performance, and David Palmer was our publicist; they were both hospitable and practical at the same time in making arrangements for us.

Since we opened with a gala – a charity affair with the proceeds going to the Royal Academy of Dancing and the Cecchetti Society – we had to engage guest artists. Marcia Haydée and Richard Cragun from the Stuttgart Ballet obliged with a spectacular Cranko pas de deux entitled *Légende* to music by H. Wieniawski; Niels Kehlet from the Royal Danish Ballet partnered Veronica Tennant in *La Sylphide*. Erik Bruhn was there to coach Niels and generally encourage us. Betty Oliphant took a holiday from the school so that she could be with us on this important occasion. Real trees were set in the foyer of the Coliseum, and flowers bedecked the royal box, to be occupied by Princess Anne and Edward Heath, then the prime minister. In the audience and at the champagne party later on the stage were Dame Marie Rambert, Dame Ninette de Valois, Sir Frederick Ashton, and Sir Robert Helpmann; old friends like Dame Alicia Markova, Beryl Grey, Leo and Janet Kersley, Mary Munro (who had taught *Winter Night* to Grant Strate and me on a visit to London years before) and her husband Brian Taylor, Honor Frost, and Cyril Frankel turned up during the run.

The program opened with *The Mirror Walkers*, partly a gesture to Britain's Royal Ballet (its choreographer, Peter Wright, was an associate director to Kenneth MacMillan); but the work also displayed the talent of our corps de ballet and was a good vehicle for our blossoming young soloists, Mary Jago, Sergiu Stefanschi, Karen Kain, and Frank Augustyn. We followed with *Légende* and then *La Sylphide*. For the role of Madge the Witch in the latter, I had to wear a hideous make-up and my hands were covered with dirty brown and grey greasepaint. Since I did not want to ruin a pair of royal kid gloves when I met Princess Anne at the stage party, I bought a cheap pair of white cotton gloves at Woolworths and so managed to look not only hideous but also ridiculous. Princess Anne was beautiful and gracious to us all; she said that it wouldn't have mattered to her about the gloves. Stanislas Idzikowski and his wife were both bursting with pride and pleasure; Rambert kept repeating 'Such a splendid company'; and de Valois, who had stayed despite a raging toothache, said in her familiar clipped voice, 'Well, dear, you did it.'

There was no doubt about the company's artistic and box office success in London. Although I had been warned not to take coals to Newcastle – i.e., not to bring any classical works – I did not see how a ballet company could be properly evaluated if critics and audience could not see it dancing the classics. Thus *Swan Lake* and *La Sylphide* were in our repertoire, and they drew the largest attendances.

We also took a wide range of modern and very modern works. Eliot Feld's deliciously romantic and fiendishly difficult *Intermezzo* to piano waltzes and intermezzi by Brahms played on stage was well danced and received. When we went on to Stuttgart, John Cranko and his dancers were particularly impressed by it. For fans of Antony Tudor we presented his *Judgment of Paris* and his *Fandango,* the latter of which was quite new to English audiences. *Session* was a jazz ballet, choreographed by Robert Iscove who later achieved fame for his work in the film 'Jesus Christ Superstar,' and set to music

Scenes from *Kraanerg*. From left to right: Veronica Tennant; Lynn Seymour with Georges Piletta; and Piletta in a spectacular leap. Below, the final peaceful scene when the boys slowly swayed the girls from side to side

by a popular Canadian composer, Doug Riley. Unfortunately, the movements in this work were so violent that dancers were often injured.

There was also *Evocation*, a pleasant 'dancy' ballet staged by Daniel Seillier; it was based on a work by William Dollar called *Constantia* and danced to Chopin's second piano concerto. Daniel had maintained the work while maître de ballet for the International Ballet du Marquis de Cuevas in Paris from 1951 to 1961. He joined our school and company in 1965, and his professional experience continues to serve us well.

And then there was *Kraanerg* – as modern as modern could be. It was commissioned for the opening of Ottawa's beautiful National Arts Centre in June 1969. The director general of the NAC, Hamilton Southam, had asked for a work as new as the Arts Centre itself – and he got it! Roland Petit choreographed it in an ultra avant-garde manner and Iannis

Xenakis composed it, using both live and taped electronic music without any recognizable beat. The sound was often ear-splitting, and at one point in the score one could rely on some members of the audience getting up and walking out. The stunning décor was by Victor Vasarely and Yvaral. We had opened it in Ottawa with Lynn Seymour from the Royal Ballet and Georges Piletta from the Paris Opéra; we even had a guest conductor, Lukas Foss, music director of the Buffalo Philharmonic Orchestra. The work certainly put paid to the myth that the National Ballet could not dance modern choreography.

Roland Petit had structured the ballet so that several dancers had exposed solos or pas de deux or pas de trois; the group work used simple stage patterns and was all the more effective for that. The English critics were not enthusiastic about the ballet itself, but agreed that we had performed it well. Dame Alicia Markova

More from the visually spectacular *Kraanerg*. Right, Timothy Spain is standing on Georges Piletta. Below, a pas de trois with Karen Bowes, Mary Jago, and Georges Piletta; below right, David Gordon, Andrew Oxenham, and Veronica Tennant. The scenes on the facing page show the eye-dazzling backdrop of narrow black and white stripes, against which various cubes and circles floated and intermingled

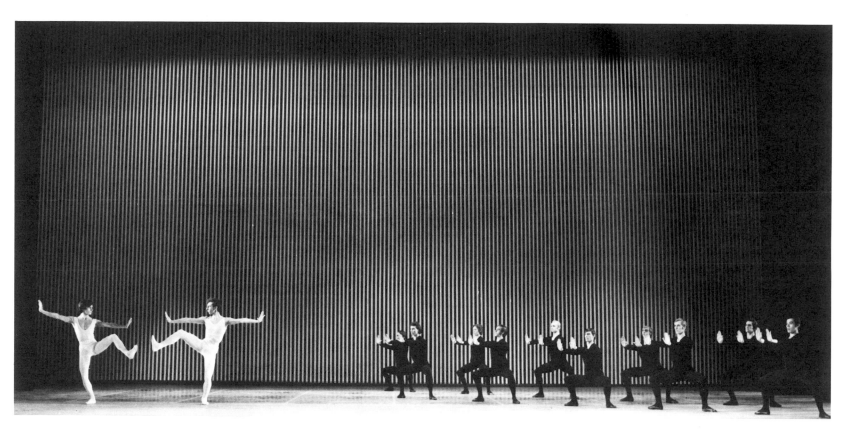

Right, the final group from the first scene of *Kraanerg*. Below, a shot taken at a rehearsal before the final touches had been made to the sphere. Below right, Piletta and Seymour are reflected in a huge floating mirror

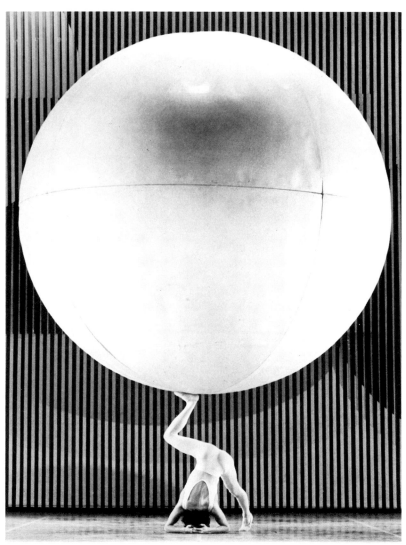

asked particularly that I present her to Mary Jago who had successfully taken over Lynn Seymour's role.

After London, we went on to Glasgow, Brussels, Stuttgart, Lausanne, Monte Carlo (where the company was stiffly entertained to dinner by Prince Rainier and Princess Grace), and Paris. The Parisians, with their self-sufficient idea of French culture, could not be described as having flocked to see us, but the critics were approving. All in all, however, the tour seemed to everyone to have been a success, and two further European trips have been undertaken since then.

That our first European tour was so successful and indeed pleasurable was due in large part to the work of our managers and support staff. David Haber was 'loaned' to us by the National Arts Centre when our general manager, Wallace Russell, suddenly left us in March just before the tour. Our publicity director, Joe Lewis, worked most

effectively with David 'Pinkie' Palmer and he made sure that news of our activities was received back in Canada. Johnson Ashley had, thanks to a recommendation from Jean Roberts, become our company manager in 1966, and for some nine years was a great source of comfort to all of us; if anyone could charm a restaurant to stay open for us after a show, it was Johnson. Dieter Penzhorn, our production manager with first-class technical knowledge, his stage managers William Warnke and Lawrence Beevers, James Ronaldson, the wardrobe supervisor with the ugliest temper and the most lovable nature, Daisy Dean, our wardrobe mistress – all worked cheerfully, competently, and conscientiously. My own assistant, David Walker, was a rock of reliability and remains to this day one of my best friends. There can be no greater joy than working with such skilful and compatible colleagues.

While all the excitement of the first tour was building up in

Canada, we had also been dealing with another 'big time' offer. In March 1971, our general manager, Wally Russell, told me that he had had a meeting with Sol Hurok, the New York impresario, who was envisaging a long tour of the United States, with performances in the top theatres climaxing with a season in the Metropolitan Opera House in New York; Nureyev was to be the 'guest star,' and the company would have to produce and pay for a Nureyev version of *The Sleeping Beauty* with designs by Nicholas Georgiadis. Nureyev was to dance seven performances per week, and Hurok would pay the company a guaranteed weekly fee and all travelling and promotion costs.

Our artistic management committee met to consider the proposal. Where would the money come from to produce *Beauty*? How would our own male dancers develop if Rudi took the leading role in every performance? I liked the idea because, with the excep-

tion of Centennial Year, our dancers had never had the chance to perform steadily for months on end. We were too long in rehearsal rooms for lack of funds, and there were often long lay-offs. Instead of feeling like a familiar home, a stage was frightening foreign territory, and the audiences were strangers. The dancers were not practising their craft enough and consequently they lacked confidence and 'attack.' We had been criticized for this, but in truth the company was only half its age since we were not performing in most seasons for more than half a year. Now the company could make the progress and acquire the experience which it could obtain only through more frequent and repeated performances.

This production of *Sleeping Beauty* would also have the advantage of increasing the company to at least sixty dancers, as I had long wanted. In 1969 or so we had reached fifty-five, but we had had to cut back to about forty. For our large productions – *Romeo and Juliet, The Nutcracker, Cinderella, Kraanerg,* for example – we were able to call upon the students at the school to augment the company in and around Toronto, but we could not tour extensively with the students. Extra dancers would help in all our other classical productions, and indeed in establishing our international reputation in the forthcoming tour to Europe.

Sol Hurok insisted that negotiations be kept confidential, so the artistic management committee agreed not to inform the executive committee for the time being and to send Wally Russell and myself to Buenos Aires to talk with Nureyev, who was rehearsing his production of *The Nutcracker* there. One of Hurok's vice presidents, Sheldon Gold, was waiting there for us, contract in hand! He seemed to think we should sign at once, but it struck me that the course of discretion was to talk to Nureyev first and let the lawyers on our board have a look at the terms of the contract. 'Oh, what have you done to me?' Sheldon lamented that first evening.

The next day I had lunch with Rudi to go over his ideas for the production and to find out his casting requirements; there were to be armies of supernumeraries! I could imagine too, since I had seen Georgiadis' scenery for the Royal Ballet's version of *Romeo and Juliet,* that we would be letting ourselves in for unprecedented expenditures on the décor. Rudi and Niko said they intended basing our *Sleeping Beauty* on one they had mounted at La Scala: it was of 'magnitudinous' proportions and planned to be firmly secured to the stage for a long, unbroken run. Though vaguely suspicious, we did not worry unduly, for after all this was to be a touring production and we expected to receive designs to suit such circumstances. But there was no sign of restraint: Rudi and Niko started ordering outrageously

The sets for *The Lesson* were wonderfully effective in creating a dance studio, in which the Teacher eventually strangles the Pupil. Murray Kilgour as the Teacher and Veronica Tennant are seen in rehearsal at the right; below, Fleming Flindt, the choreographer, as the Teacher; below right, Tennant and Flint and Celia Franca as the Pianist. Opposite, Veronica's toes are hurting – the fanatical Teacher has been overworking her; the pas de deux; and the final murder

extravagant items like massive specially constructed chandeliers, several coaches for the hunting party, and scrims galore for transformations. When they found themselves together in London, they chose the most lavish fabrics for the costumes – all regardless of expense.

Wally Russell had been dealing with Nureyev and Georgiadis until his sudden departure in March 1972. During my first week in London on our European tour that year, Dieter Penzhorn and I had gone to see Niko and asked him to cut down the number of flying pieces, construction pieces, costumes for the supernumeraries, and so on. He replied that he had been asked to design the décor to fit the largest stage of the National Arts Centre in Ottawa and that Rudi, now in another part of the world, had said that he could not choreograph for fewer 'supers.' The NAC stage, however, was larger than any other booked on the tour, apart from that in the Metropolitan Opera House, and even there the

sheer volume of the scenery and effects being planned could never be fitted into the storage areas. Finally, we succeeded in having only one chandelier, only one coach, fewer scrims, and fewer costumes; but the original cost estimate of $250 000 was far exceeded by the time this *Sleeping Beauty* was premiered in Ottawa in September 1972.

All things considered, however, this production was beneficial for the company. The dancers met new choreographic challenges, and Karen Kain and Frank Augustyn partnered one another divinely in the pas de deux of the Bluebird and Princess Florine. This was one of the pas de deux they took to the International Ballet Competition in Moscow the following June. At the last session of the jury (of which I was a member), Irina Kolpakova, the lovely ballerina of the Kirov Ballet, nominated Karen and Frank for the prize for the best duet. Their 'Bluebird' was one of the great highlights of the competition, and

Gary Norman as the Prince in the vision scene from *The Sleeping Beauty*

The Rose Adagio, with Veronica Tennant and Hazaros Surmeyan

250

Scenes from *The Sleeping Beauty*: right,
Veronica Tennant is held aloft by her
suitors in the Rose Adagio; below,
Nureyev and Tennant in the grand pas de
deux from Act III (two photographs);
opposite, the vision scene, with the artists
of the ballet as Naiads

A palatial production of *Don Juan*

there was not a single dissenting voice over this award. Eugen Valukin from the Bolshoi Ballet, a frequent guest teacher with the company and school, was most kind to us in Moscow and had helped coach Karen and Frank; he made some significant suggestions, for which we were particularly grateful since, owing to our tour schedule, there had been little time for special coaching before leaving for Moscow.

The North American tour was in two parts: after the opening in Ottawa we travelled to Montreal and through the eastern States until mid-October; we then played our usual three-week season in Toronto, with Nureyev dancing Prince Florimund in *Beauty* for the first week and Frank Augustyn for the final week. The tour resumed in February 1973 with Nureyev at Vancouver and ended, after performances in twenty-one cities in the States, at New York with three weeks in the Met. In many of the towns and cities we visited, we

could not, of course, show *Beauty* at all, such were the epic dimensions of the production.

These rounds of steady performances were just what I wanted for the company – they increased confidence and projection and they spread our reputation. Despite the worry about the initial costs of *Sleeping Beauty*, I believe that the investment was recovered in the end. The company has made similar large American tours almost every year since then; the Hurok-Nureyev performances were very much our calling card, but in the 1977-78 season the company danced in New York without Nureyev and was received with great appreciation.

When considered alongside the company's visits to Europe, these tours were all welcome realizations of my dreams. We had become known and admired not only in Canada but in the ballet centres of the western world. The only regret is that the whole company has not yet danced to the receptive

*Don Juan* is a ballet pantomime first produced in Vienna in 1761 to music by Gluck and much revived during this century. These photographs of the NBC production show Rudolf Nureyev and Sergiu Stefanschi both playing the Don with a variety of partners

Top, left to right: some of the characters from the 1974 production of John Neumeier's version of *Don Juan*: Karen Kain as Aminta, Vanessa Harwood as Dona Aña, Mary Jago as the Lady in White and Nureyev as the Don, Veronica Tennant as Dona Aña. Bottom, left to right: Sergiu Stefanschi and Vanessa Harwood; Winthrop Corey as Catalinón acts the part of the Don in a 'play within a play'; Tennant, Schramek, Kain, and Nureyev in a jealous scene

audiences of the USSR – but there
are reasons within reasons why
that has not yet happened. Karen
Kain and Frank Augustyn were,
however, invited to dance in Russia
and that I take as some recognition
of the quality that has been attain-
ed in Canadian ballet. And I know
now that the company would receive
a warm welcome in China.

*Envoi*

As the company had grown in size and popularity, there had also, of course, been a great increase in the work that I as artistic director was supposed to do. I was pulled in too many directions and was criticized for not paying enough attention to the dancers, or the volunteers, or the fund-raisers, or the media, or some other group of people important in our life. I had therefore been keeping an eye open for someone who could share the tasks involved in the artistic direction of the company. Just as it was necessary to establish a school to ensure the continuity of the company, so was it important for the company's future to establish some continuity and development in its artistic direction.

Thus it was a great relief to me in 1973 when David Haber agreed to take on the position of co-director. We worked together for a year while David became acclimatized and learned about us and our methods. When it seemed that he was ready to assume full responsibility, I stepped down, abandoning the title of artistic director but continuing to work as a kind of minister without portfolio. I looked forward to a long overdue sabbatical, comfortable in the thought that the company was in good hands.

In June 1975 I heard that David had been asked to resign; this he did as of the end of July 1975 – a most inopportune time, since our (by now) annual summer engagement in New York was upon us and the twenty-fifth anniversary season was coming up. After having been part of the company's growth for so long, I could not happily face the uncertainties of its appearing in New York without a 'leader.' Once again I was the director, at least until the end of September when we would have concluded our Montreal engagement with Baryshnikov.

A search committee for a new artistic director was established by the board when it asked Haber to resign. It was clear to me, though I was never formally asked, that I had

Karen Bowes and Hazaros Surmeyan in
*Romeo and Juliet*, and Galina Samtsova
as Juliet

Scenes from Sir Frederick Ashton's
enchanting *La Fille mal gardée*

12 November 1976: for the twenty-fifth anniversary performance of *Romeo and Juliet*, Celia Franca was invited to play Lady Capulet, here being carried off with the dead Tybalt

to hand in my resignation from the company too, since it would be inhibiting for a new director to have the founder hanging around in the wings. I knew the search committee would have a hard enough time finding and obtaining a suitable director and I didn't want to add to their problems.

Alexander Grant, one of the world's finest character dancers from the Royal Ballet in London, accepted the board's invitation and paid several visits to see the artists and administration before officially taking on the position of artistic director on 1 July 1976. It was a fortunate appointment, for Alexander was able, through his friendship with Sir Frederick Ashton, to obtain a number of his lovely ballets. *La Fille mal gardée* was the perfect addition to the repertoire in that season of celebration. The season opened at the O'Keefe centre twenty-five years to the day after our début at the Eaton auditorium in 1951: Veronica Tennant and Frank Augustyn danced the title roles in *Romeo and Juliet.*

Besides the performances, the anniversary was marked by an international dance seminar sponsored by the Canada Council. Many people from the ballet world and friends old and new attended these events: Sir Fred himself, Dame Ninette de Valois, Erik Bruhn, Pearl Whitehead, Betty Oliphant, Lois Smith, Earl Kraul, Angela Leigh, Walter Foster, Ludmilla Chiriaeff, Arnold Spohr, Clive Barnes, Margaret Dale, Peter Brinson, John Percival, William Littler; and many others. The new secretary of state, John Roberts, spoke from the stage at the end of the opening performance and presented me with a framed scroll after the president of the board, Paul Deacon, had read its message. There were more speeches at the Toronto city hall where the city council held a reception. In the excitement, I lost my carry-all bag – or was it my white mink jacket, or both? – but Charlotte ('Charley Horse') Holmes, the company's former executive secretary, found it.

For many of us, the most moving event occurred two days later at the Sunday matinée performance of *Romeo and Juliet.* Yves Cousineau, who had joined the dance department at York University some years before, was invited back to play Tybalt, and Lilian Jarvis returned to dance Juliet to Hazaros Surmeyan's Romeo. All the former members of the company from 1951 onwards whom we could locate were invited to attend the performance, make an appearance on stage at the end, and join in a happy supper reunion. There was much laughter and 'many a tear was shed'; old colleagues recognized and hugged each other and exchanged stories and gossip; Hamilton ('Tony') Cassels Jr, a son-in-law of Aileen Woods and over the years a supporter, a board member, and· president of the board, skipped happily from table to table taking photographs of all the celebrants. When times had been rough, he had often tried to cheer me – and I

suspect himself – by quoting the old saying, 'Onwards and Upwards.'

Perhaps this is as fitting a motto for the second quarter century of the company as it was for the first.

*On the Photography*

My first contact with the National Ballet was an assignment from *Maclean's* magazine to photograph the fledgling company during its first rehearsals and presentations. In 1951 my knowledge of ballet was very limited, but the attraction of this young and struggling company and the magic of the ballet itself proved difficult to resist. There were several assignments from other magazines and before long I found myself becoming the official photographer to the National Ballet – a role I filled for almost twenty-five years.

As Celia has written earlier in this book, there was little money in those early days; and this was true for many years to come. My rewards came rather from working in this exciting new medium of Canadian theatre and in being free to express through photography the visual poetry and beauty of the dances.

To start with, photographs were all taken with a Rolleiflex, a twin-lens reflex camera which had been my favourite through the Second World War and continued so into the 1950s. It was a great camera for most kinds of work, but it was limiting for the ballet since it had only one focal length.

The introduction of the Hasselblad camera, with its many interchangeable lenses and its unlimited (except by one's budget) number of film magazines, started a new era in photography. The range of focal-length lenses allowed one to take photographs from any part of the theatre desired or required; one could work from the wings, for example, as well as from the balcony, and with a wide-angle lens include the whole stage or company or by then changing to a longer focal-length lens, centre in on the principals. With its several film magazines, it was possible to change from black-and-white film to colour film or to colour negative without missing an appreciable part of the performance.

The Hasselblad still had its limitations, however. Even with the increasing speed of both black-

An ethereal Martine van Hamel
as La Sylphide

Swan Maidens shot from high above the stage during a performance

and-white and colour film, the shutter speed of such a larger-format camera was too slow to catch an unblurred image of any quick action on stage or at rehearsals. And the noise of the mirror tripping was disturbing to audiences and dancers. Though such a 2¼-inch single-lens reflex camera is still ideal for photo-calls in a theatre or for studio shots, its use was supplemented in the early 1960s by such new and smaller cameras as the 35mm SLR Nikon, Canon, and Leica. Their shutter speed was faster and they were much quieter and easier to handle; with one camera loaded with black-and-white film and another with colour film, a photographer shooting from a tripod could overcome most problems.

The only remaining difficulty was caused by the small size of the negative or transparency: when enlarged to any size, the reproduction would appear grainy, though this could be partially offset by the greater depth of field. With new and better film, however, grain became less and less of a problem. But, to begin with, newspapers and magazines commissioning colour photographs of ballets insisted on having 8 x 10 transparencies with a studio camera in order to reduce the grain. This was a difficult and expensive process, but now the print media are happy to use photographs from the smaller-size cameras, with little or no loss in quality and large gains in speed, sharpness, selection, and cost.

Thus the ideal arrangement today is to have both types of camera – the larger Hasselblad and the 35mm – and to use them according to circumstances – from publicity shots in a studio to live-action shots in the theatre – and the type of ballet or action being photographed. No two situations are exactly the same, and one has to be prepared for any eventuality.

The earlier photographs were taken mostly with available light, though sometimes flashbulbs on extension cords were used to gain

A multiple exposure of Veronica Tennant

modelling from the lighting. Again, as with the introduction of the new and more versatile cameras, the electronic flash changed photograph techniques: instead of taking so many posed photographs, it became possible to have the dancers leaping through the air and still 'stop' the action completely. This produced some exciting results.

The early studio shots of leaping dancers had been constrained by the size of the background. In those days a nine-foot roll of coloured no-seam paper was placed on a studio wall and curved on to the floor; against such a limited width, it was not uncommon to find a good shot ruined by a hand or a foot or even a head coming outside the area of the backdrop. For a large group, I'd put up two or more rolls side by side and then, faced with the problem of the join between the rolls showing on the photograph, try to have a dancer in such a position that he or she covered as much of the seam as possible.

These studio problems were eventually overcome, as the company increased in size and more and more photographs were required, by altering a whole wall of the studio so that it curved invisibly at the bottom and later at the top, thus eliminating any line on the photographs between floor, wall, and ceiling; the wall was then painted in the desired colour of fast-drying latex paint. This feature is now almost a necessity in all professional studios.

In time, too, the use of the electronic flash gave way to the use of tungsten lighting, with which it was much easier to create a mood and which, even at high speed, could allow just enough blurring to a hand or foot to create a feeling of dancing and movement rather than of a static cut-out. As tungsten incandescent) lighting was used in all theatres, this made essential the use of small-format cameras. In the theatre, after all, the photographer has to catch the mood of the dance, in part created by the lighting; it is not like studio photography where

the photographer can use lights to create his own mood or style.

Catching a moment in a stage performance is not easy; one has to know one's cameras so well that no time is necessary to stop and think before shooting; and one has to know the ballet and develop a sense of timing so that one can anticipate the action. Then a photographer can feel the beat of the music, knowing that the dancer is going to reach the peak of a jeté on a certain beat in a certain place, then shoot.

I hope that these brief thoughts will help the reader and the viewer of this book to some understanding of how the different photographs were taken. For my part, however, I do not recall these days in terms only of technique; I remember also the apparent chaos of my studio when dancers were preparing for studio shots: clothes and make-up everywhere, tutus hanging from doors, the coffee pot always on – an exciting, warm, comfortable, and creative little part of the world.

I would like to express my thanks to everyone in the company who has helped me through the years. Dancers, stage hands, public relation personnel, and musicians were all friendly and co-operative. Particularly do I thank Celia Franca and Kay Ambrose – perfectionists both, so kind and yet so tough. I am pleased to acknowledge the assistance of Peter Croydon, who took several of the earlier photographs, and to other photographers who worked for me on photographing the National Ballet of Canada. The Public Archives of Canada, which now holds thousands of these photographs, was most co-operative in assisting in the preparation of the photographs I chose for this book; the fine eye of Will Rueter was responsible for much of the final selection. And to my production and darkroom staff who produced these thousands of prints and also maintained a high standard of quality over these twenty-five years, my lasting thanks.

KEN BELL

*A List of the Ballets*

This listing records the ballets produced each season by the National Ballet of Canada from 1951 to the summer of 1976. It includes television productions but omits short items taken from longer works. Hyphens between the names of choreographers means that each contributed; a solidus means that the first-named choreographer adapted the work of the second; a name in parentheses means that that choreographer staged the work according to notation of the work of the first-named choreographer.

| | BALLET | CHOREOGRAPHER | DESIGNER | COMPOSER |
|---|---|---|---|---|
| FIRST SEASON (1951-52) | *Les Sylphides* | Fokine | Pape | Chopin |
| | *The Dance of Salome* | Franca | Hall/Budner | Hartley |
| | *Etude* | Armstrong | Armstrong | Tchaikovsky |
| | *Polovtsian Dances* | Fokine | Mess/Lett | Borodin |
| | *Giselle* II | Coralli – Perrot – Petipa | Ambrose | Adam |
| | *Ballet Composite* | Adams | Adams | Brahms |
| | *The Nutcracker* II | Franca/Petipa | Rose | Tchaikovsky |
| | *L'Après-midi d'un faune* | Franca | Ambrose | Debussy |
| | *Ballet behind Us* | Adams | Mess | |
| | *Coppélia* II | Saint-Léon | Pape | Delibes |
| SECOND SEASON (1952-53) | *Coppélia* I *and* II | Saint-Léon | Ambrose/Pape | Delibes |
| | *Giselle (complete)* | Corrali – Perrot – Petipa | Ambrose | Adam |
| | *Le Pommier* | Franca | Ambrose | Gratton |
| | *Jardin aux lilas* | Tudor | Ambrose | Chausson |
| THIRD SEASON (1953-54) | *Swan Lake* II | Petipa – Ivanov | Ambrose | Tchaikovsky |
| | *Gala Performance* | Tudor | Ambrose | Prokofiev |
| | *Dark of the Moon (Barbara Allen)* | Harris | Ambrose | Applebaum |
| | *Dances from the Classics* | | Ambrose | Tchaikovsky |

Joanne Nisbet (seated), Betty Oliphant,
David Scott, Daniel Seillier, and James
the beagle

David Walker

| | BALLET | CHOREOGRAPHER | DESIGNER | COMPOSER |
|---|---|---|---|---|
| **FOURTH SEASON (1954-55)** | *Swan Lake (complete; 4 acts)* | Petipa – Ivanov | Ambrose | Tchaikovsky |
| | *Offenbach in the Underworld* | Tudor | Ambrose | Offenbach |
| **FIFTH SEASON (1955-56)** | *The Nutcracker (complete)* | Franca/Petipa | Rose | Tchaikovsky |
| | *Dark Elegies* | Tudor | Benois | Mahler |
| | *The Lady from the Sea* | Leese | Belleval | Honigman |
| **SIXTH SEASON (1956-57)** | *Giselle (complete; 2nd version)* | Coralli – Perrot – Petipa | Ambrose | Adam |
| | *Les Rendez-vous* | Ashton | Chappell | Auber |
| | *The Fisherman and His Soul* | Strate | Ambrose | Somers |
| | *La Llamada* | Moller | de Villalonga | Gomez |
| | *Post Script* | MacDonald | | Morrow |
| | *Pas de chance* | Adams | Ambrose | Tchaikovsky |
| | *Swan Lake (TV)* | | | |
| **SEVENTH SEASON (1957-58)** | *Le Carnaval* | Fokine | Ambrose/Bakst | Schumann |
| | *Winter Night* | Gore | Ambrose | Rachmaninov |
| | *The Willow* | Strate | Pittson | Foote |
| | *Dances from the Sleeping Beauty* | Franca/Petipa | Ambrose | Tchaikovsky |
| | *Coppélia (TV)* | | | |
| | *Winter Night (TV)* | | | |

George MacPherson

| | BALLET | CHOREOGRAPHER | DESIGNER | COMPOSER |
|---|---|---|---|---|
| **EIGHTH SEASON** (1958-59) | *Coppélia (complete)* | Saint-Léon | Ambrose | Délibes |
| | *Ballad* | Strate | Negin | Somers |
| | *The Nutcracker (TV)* | | | |
| **NINTH SEASON** (1959-60) | *Pineapple Poll* | Cranko | Rose | Prokofiev |
| | *Pineapple Poll (TV)* | | | |
| | *The Mermaid* | Howard | Ambrose | Ravel |
| | *Death and the Maiden* | Howard | Howard | Schubert |
| | *The Littlest One* | Adams | MacLennan | Beckwith |
| **TENTH SEASON** (1960-61) | *Princess Aurora* | Franca/Petipa | Ambrose | Tchaikovsky |
| | *Barbara Allen* (2nd version) | Adams | Ambrose | Applebaum |
| | *Antic Spring* | Strate | Negin | Ibert |
| | *Pas de six* | Adams | Ambrose | Tchaikovsky |
| | *The Remarkable Rocket* | Gillies | Nichols | Surdin |
| | *Swan Lake (TV tape: broadcast December 1961)* | | | |
| **ELEVENTH SEASON** (1961-62) | *Concerto Barocco* | Balanchine | Ambrose | Bach |
| | *One in Five* | Powell | Rencher | Strauss/Crum |
| | *Giselle (TV tape: broadcast December 1962)* | | | |

Mary McDonald

| | BALLET | CHOREOGRAPHER | DESIGNER | COMPOSER |
|---|---|---|---|---|
| **TWELFTH SEASON (1962-63)** | *Serenade* | Balanchine | Jackson | Tchaikovsky |
| | *Sequel* | Strate | Negin | Webern |
| | *Time Cycle* | Strate | Negin | Foss |
| | *Judgment of Paris* | Tudor | Laing | Weil |
| | *Pas de six from Laurencia* | Samtsova/ Chabukiane | Procur | Krein/Crum |
| | *One in Five* (TV tape: broadcast May 1964) | | | |
| **THIRTEENTH SEASON (1963-64)** | *Romeo and Juliet* | Cranko | Rose | Prokofiev |
| | *The House of Atreus* | Strate | Town | Somers |
| | *Allégresse* | Solov | Doyle | Mendelssohn |
| **FOURTEENTH SEASON (1964-65)** | *The Nutcracker* | Franca/Petipa | Rose | Tchaikovsky |
| | *Triptych* | Strate | | Mozart |
| | *Electre* | Strate | Rose | Pousseur |
| | *La Sylphide* | Bruhn/ Bournonville | Prévost | Løvenskjold/Crum |
| | *Romeo and Juliet* (TV tape: broadcast September 1965) | | | |
| **FIFTEENTH SEASON (1965-66)** | *Pulcinella* | Strate | Negin | Stravinsky |
| | *Rake's Progress* | de Valois (Worth) | Whistler/ Hogarth/Schafer | Gordon |
| | *Rivalité* | Seillier | | Rossini |
| | *Solitaire* | MacMillan (Worth) | Schafer | Arnold |
| | *Adagio Cantabile* | Poll | | Albinoni |

Grant Strate

| | BALLET | CHOREOGRAPHER | DESIGNER | COMPOSER |
|---|---|---|---|---|
| **SIXTEENTH SEASON (1966-67)** | *Bayaderka IV* | Valukin/Petipa | | Minkus |
| | *Swan Lake* | Bruhn/Petipa | Heeley | Tchaikovsky |
| | *Eh! (ballet concert)* | Franca | Schafer | Poulenc |
| | *Rondo Giocoso (ballet concert)* | Poll | Schafer | Rossini |
| | *Swan Lake (TV tape: broadcast December 1967)* | | | |
| **SEVENTEENTH SEASON (1967-68)** | *Cinderella* | Franca | Rose | Prokofiev |
| | *La Prima Ballerina* | Heiden | Schafer | Ridout |
| | *Studies in White* | Strate | Schafer | Telemann |
| | *Cinderella (TV tape: broadcast December 1968)* | | | |
| **EIGHTEENTH SEASON (1968-69)** | *Kraanerg* | Petit | Vasarely/Yvaral | Xenakis |
| | *Cyclus* | Strate | Bogaerts | Welffens |
| | *Four Temperaments* | Balanchine | | Hindemith |
| | *Phases* | Strate | | Satie |
| | *Celebrations (ballet concert)* | Poll | Schafer | Fauré |
| | *The Arena (ballet concert)* | Strate | Bogaerts | Britten |
| **NINETEENTH SEASON (1969-70)** | *Giselle (3rd version)* | Wright/Coralli – Perrot – Petipa | Heeley | Adam |
| | *Le Loup* | Petit | Carzou | Dutilleux |
| | *The Lesson (Ionesco)* | Flindt | Daydé | Delerue |

Victoria Polly

| | BALLET | CHOREOGRAPHER | DESIGNER | COMPOSER |
|---|---|---|---|---|
| **TWENTIETH SEASON (1970-71)** | *Brown Earth* | Ditchburn | King | Nyro/King/Goffin |
| | *For Internal Use as Well* | Spain | | Mills-Cockell |
| | *Sagar* | Spain | | Subotnick |
| | *The Mirror Walkers* | Wright | | Tchaikovsky |
| **TWENTY-FIRST SEASON (1971-72)** | *Fandango* | Tudor | Laing | Soler |
| | *Evocation* | Seillier/Dollar | | Chopin |
| | *Intermezzo* | Feld | Simmons | Brahms |
| | *Session* | Iscove | Marki | Riley |
| **TWENTY-SECOND SEASON (1972-73)** | *Sleeping Beauty* | Nureyev | Georgiadis | Tchaikovsky |
| | *Sleeping Beauty (TV tape: broadcast December 1972)* | | | |
| | *The Moor's Pavane* | Limon | Lawrence | Purcell |
| **TWENTY-THIRD SEASON (1973-74)** | *Les Sylphides (2nd version)* | Franca and Bruhn/ Fokine | Farmer | Chopin/Crum |
| | *Don Juan* | Neumeier | Sanjust | Gluck |
| **TWENTY-FOURTH SEASON (1974-75)** | *Coppélia (2nd version)* | Bruhn | Strike | Delibes |
| | *Inventions* | Patsalas | Patsalas | Kabelac |
| | *Kettentanz* | Arpino | Eula | Strauss Sr /Mayer |
| | *Whispers of Darkness* | Vesak | Lee | Mahler |
| | *Giselle (TV tape: broadcast November 1976)* | | | |

George Crum

| BALLET | CHOREOGRAPHER | DESIGNER | COMPOSER |
|---|---|---|---|
| *Offenbach in the Underworld (revival)* | Tudor | Ambrose | Offenbach/Crum |
| *Kisses* | Ditchburn | Ditchburn | Contemporary |
| *Monument for a Dead Boy* | van Dantzig | van Schayk | Boerman |

TWENTY-FIFTH SEASON (1975-76)

This book
was designed by
WILLIAM RUETER
was set in type by
MONO LINO TYPESETTING
COMPANY LIMITED
was printed by
McLAREN MORRIS AND TODD LIMITED
and was bound by
THE HUNTER ROSE COMPANY LTD
for the
University of
Toronto
Press